# NAMA-JAPA
# IN THE YOGA OF TRANSFORMATION

SRI RAMKRISHNA DAS

PRISMA

# ACKNOWLEDGEMENTS

All texts and photos are the property of
Sri Aurobindo Ashram Trust, Pondicherry.

Book : NAMA-JAPA - IN THE YOGA OF TRANSFORMATION
Language : English

Author : SRI RAMKRISHNA DAS
Copyright: Auro Seva Trust

ISBN 978-93-95460-73-6 (print)
ISBN 978-93-95460-48-4 (ebook)

BISAC Code:
OCC000000   BODY, MIND & SPIRIT / General
OCC010000   BODY, MIND & SPIRIT / Mindfulness & Meditation
OCC014000   BODY, MIND & SPIRIT / New Thought
EDU040000   EDUCATION / Philosophy, Theory & Social Aspects
PHI000000   PHILOSOPHY / General
PHI003000   PHILOSOPHY / Eastern
PHI015000   PHILOSOPHY / Mind & Body
PSY000000   PSYCHOLOGY / General
SEL000000   SELF-HELP / General
SEL032000   SELF-HELP / Spiritual
REL062000   RELIGION / Spirituality

Thema Subject Category:
QD Philosophy
VS Self-help, personal development and practical advice
VX Mind, body, spirit
VXM Mind, body, spirit: meditation and visualization

Cataloging-in-Publication Data for this title is available from the
Library of Congress.

PRISMA, an imprint of Digital Media Initiatives
PRISMA, Aurelec / Prayogshala,
Auroville 605101, Tamil Nadu, Indiaa
www.prisma.haus

# Contents

| | |
|---|---:|
| Publisher's Note | |
| Sri Ramkrishna Das | |
| The Role of Nama-Japa in the Yoga of Transformation | 1 |
| Nama-Japa in Work | 9 |
| The Mother on Japa | 12 |
| Nama-Japa in Worldly Life | 14 |
| Nama-Japa Can Remove Obstacles and Dangers | 18 |
| Questions and Answers | 22 |
| Obstacles and Hindrances | 36 |
|    Anger | 36 |
|    Lust | 39 |
|    Ego and Selfishness | 42 |
| Harmony in Collective Work | 47 |
| Causes of Disharmony | 49 |
| The Mother's Inspiration from Within | 54 |
| Attacks from the Hostile Forces in the Process of Transformation | 56 |
| The Methods of Nama-Japa | 65 |
| The Effect of *Ma*-Nama-Japa | 67 |
| Meditation | 70 |
| The Greatness of Nama-Japa | 73 |

## PART TWO

| | |
|---|---:|
| Introduction to Part Two | 77 |
| Babaji Maharaj Ramkrishna Das | 78 |
| The Aim of Life and Sri Aurobindo's Yoga | 83 |
| How do we begin? | 97 |
|   More from the sadhak's diary | 117 |
| Sweet Babaji Maharaj | 127 |
| The Mother and Sri Aurobindo on Nama-Japa | 141 |
| Japa and Science | 143 |
| References | 147 |
| Glossary | 150 |

# Publisher's Note

*Nama-Japa in the Yoga of Transformation* was written originally for an Indian audience and published in Oriya, one of the Indian languages. Some of the references to family life and society therefore refer specifically to the Indian setting. In the original version the author makes short references to a number of episodes from India's two great epics, the *Mahabharata* and the *Ramayana*, in order to illustrate points in the text. Since Western readers are usually unfamiliar with the wider implications of these stories, most of them have been omitted from this English translation.

Throughout this work, the spiritual seeker is referred to as 'he' and as 'the sadhak', as per convention. This is not intended to imply any discrimination between male and female aspirants.

Except for where the meaning is made clear in the text itself, the meaning of all Sanskrit terms and all English words which have a special usage or significance in Sri Aurobindo's Yoga may be found in the Glossary.

"There are two paths of Yoga, one of tapasya (discipline), and the other of surrender. The path of tapasya is arduous. Here you rely solely upon yourself, you proceed by your own strength. You ascend and achieve according to the measure of your force. There is always the danger of falling down. And once you fall, you lie broken in the abyss and there is hardly a remedy. The other path, the path of surrender, is safe and sure. It is here, however, that the Western people find their difficulty. They have been taught to fear and avoid all that threatens their personal independence. They have imbibed with their mothers' milk the sense of individuality. And surrender means giving up all that. In other words, you may follow, as Ramakrishna says, either the path of the baby monkey or that of the baby cat. The baby monkey holds to its mother in order to be carried about and it must hold firm, otherwise if it loses its grip, it falls. On the other hand, the baby cat does not hold to its mother, but is held by the mother and has no fear nor responsibility; it has nothing to do but to let the mother hold it and cry ma ma."

The Mother

* * *

"If something wrong happens, at once repeat my name – Ma, Ma."

The Mother

# Sri Ramkrishna Das

Sri Ramkrishna Das, lovingly and respectfully referred to as 'Babaji Maharaj', was born in 1908 in Rayarpur, a small village in the eastern part of Orissa, India. Already at the age of eight he had determined that as soon as he grew up, he would forsake the ordinary way of life and take up the life of a sannyasi in search of the highest Truth and he began to practise nama-japa. His resolve to realise the Divine remained firm even throughout his youth and finally, as a young adult, Babaji left the fold of his family in order to search for his guru. In the depth of his heart burned the aspiration to become the disciple of the greatest living Mahatma (spiritual master) on earth.

Babaji went to Ayodhya, in northern India, and became the disciple and personal attendant of 'Mauni Baba', a well-known realised saint. He served his guruji for many years. As part of his intensive yoga practice, Babaji repeated the name of the Lord constantly and as a result received his direct darshan on several occasions. He used to experience an unceasing stream of intense Divine Bliss while practising nama-japa.

While still in Ayodhya, Babaji eventually came into contact with the writings of Sri Aurobindo and the Mother. He realised that Sri Aurobindo's Integral Yoga was not merely the culmination of all the various paths of yoga of the past, but the beginning of something entirely new, the next step in the evolutionary advance of mankind. Sri

Aurobindo's Yoga does not aim at the transcendence of life, but at the transformation of the entire human nature, turning mind, life and body, into their divine principles, resulting in a divine life here on earth. Babaji recognised that Sri Aurobindo and the Mother were the avatars of the present age. Therefore he joined the Sri Aurobindo Ashram in Pondicherry, South-India, in 1945 and lived there for the next fifty-three years.

Babaji practised the Integral Yoga with great concentration and intensity, repeating the Mother's name continuously. After the Mother's passing in 1973, Babaji began to contemplate the importance of nama-japa in the Integral Yoga. By the light of his own experiences and through the careful study of *Mother's Agenda*, the Mother's chronological record concerning her work of transformation of the body, Babaji became convinced that the difficult goal of physical transformation was only possible by the constant repetition of the Mother's name, since only japa has a direct influence on the cells of the body.

From this time onward, Babaji advised the many seekers who came to him for guidance to repeat the Mother's name constantly, with an attitude of surrender and aspiration. He wrote thousands of letters answering the questions of seekers with regard to their sadhana and their daily life-problems and unwaveringly insisted that all should repeat the Mother's name, by which any type of problem could be overcome.

Babaji left his body on the 8$^{th}$ of November, 1998.

A western disciple of Sri Aurobindo and the Mother reports her experience when she saw Babaji for the first time:

"I met Babaji for the first time in the spring of 1984, during my first visit to the Ashram. I was waiting together with a small group of people outside Babaji's room. Suddenly the door opened and Babaji appeared holding a small green plastic pitcher in his hand. Instantly there was a pin-drop silence. Babaji glanced at the small congregation of people in front of his door and an unimaginably sweet and compassionate smile lit up his face. The moment I saw Babaji I got the 'goose-bumps' all over my body and all my body hair seemed to stand on end. Something like an electric current passed through my whole being from the top of my head to my feet and the clear words arose in my mind: *This man is all love.*"

Babaji 1998

# The Role of Nama-Japa in the Yoga of Transformation

In the Yoga of Transformation, there is only one sure and certain way to overcome all seemingly insurmountable obstacles, to pass securely through even the most cunning and subtle attacks of the hostile forces and to safely reach the goal. This way is to surrender at the feet of the Mother like a small child and repeat her name. It is never safe to tread the path of this yoga without this impenetrable armour.

The aim of this yoga is to realise the Divine in a transformed mind, vital and body and to attain complete freedom from sorrow, suffering, ignorance, disease, old age and death. This is, without exception, the true aim of life for everyone in this world. There is not a single person who wants sorrow, suffering, ignorance, disease, old age and death; but nevertheless, man has been in the grip of these afflictions from the very beginning of creation.

In the past it was not possible to realise God in the mind, vital and body. This realisation could not be attained either by means of any powerful sadhana of the traditional yogas or by any yoga-shakti. The rishis and sages of the Vedic age, and the saints and yogis of subsequent periods, could not imagine or even conceive of the transformation of the mind, vital and body. Consequently the sadhaks of the traditional yogas separated themselves from their mind, vital and body, attaining Nirvana, Liberation or Divine Realisation with the help of their antaratma (soul), which is an eternal, pure and true part of the Divine. These were individual realisations and did not cause sorrow, suffering, ignorance, darkness, hatred, ego, selfishness and falsehood to disappear from this world. On the contrary, we find that these negative qualities have gradually increased. They are, however, destined to disappear and this death-bound world will eventually be transformed into a Divine Heaven. Since the time for this change had not yet arrived, the rishis and sages of the past had not thought of such a transformation.

Mind has now reached the summit of its evolutionary development and thus the time has come for the transformation of the mind, vital and body and the establishment of the Supramental Consciousness in a transformed mind, vital and body.

In order to make this transformation possible, the Divine Sachchidananda, in accordance with his own predestined will and decree, incarnated on earth in the forms of Sri Aurobindo and the Mother. As representative of the human race and accepting the inviolable laws of this death-bound world, they did sadhana and brought down and established upon earth, the Supramental Force of Parardha – the World of Truth and Light. It is this Supramental Force that is now carrying out the work of transformation. This transformation is the aim of life for each and every human being and all human beings, both those who have faith in the

Divine and those who do not, are unknowingly marching towards this goal. But since we have not yet understood the true goal of our lives, we naturally cannot follow the correct path to achieve it and this is why we undergo ever more suffering. Now that the Mother and Sri Aurobindo have established the Supramental Force upon earth, the proper time for the transformation has arrived and we have the opportunity to attain the true aim of life.

In this Yoga of Transformation, the Mother will completely protect the sadhak from all kinds of obstacles and dangers if he depends upon her totally like a small child, surrenders at her feet and continuously repeats her name, *Ma*, with faith and dependence on her. Just as a mother keeps her child safe in her arms while crossing a dangerous road, the Mother's Power fully helps the sadhak to reach the goal and overcome every kind of obstacle and hindrance. But until the transformation is complete, the sadhak has to make a conscious surrender. A total surrender of one's being at the feet of the Mother, along with the practice of nama-japa, is the only way to reach the goal and to face and overcome obstacles and hindrances and the attacks of the adverse forces.

The Mother and Sri Aurobindo are one and the same Truth. The Mother, the Matrishakti and the transforming Supramental Force are also one and the same Truth. Just as water and waves or words and their meaning are inseparable, the Divine, Sri Aurobindo and the Mother, the Supramental Force and the name *Ma*, are also inseparable. They are different in name and expression, but in essence they are one. Since the Divine, Sri Aurobindo, the Mother and the Supramental Force are inseparable, it follows that in the Integral Yoga, when the sadhak surrenders to the Mother, the Supramental Power will begin the work of transformation in his mind, vital and body. Since the Mother and her name are the same Truth and Principle, whenever the sadhak repeats her name, the Mother's presence remains with him. The difficult sadhana of transformation becomes very easy by doing nama-japa.

It has already been said that the practice of the Integral Yoga is not safe without surrender, but genuine surrender and aspiration are possible only if the sadhak remains conscious. In order to become conscious, he has to keep up a determined willpower and maintain a continuous effort towards surrender and aspiration. The determination, however, has to be strong, the attitude towards surrender has to be intense and the sadhak has to have a burning aspiration in order to develop this state of consciousness in which the true and genuine surrender and aspiration are always possible. The sadhak must do many years of sadhana to reach such a stage. In the initial stages he has no support whatsoever for concentrating his mind and remaining constantly conscious, though he may be able to concentrate in the depths of the heart or above the head for a short while during meditation. When the sadhak surrenders, the Mother's Power starts the work of transformation, which enables him to concentrate easily. During those times when the divine qualities such as peace, concentration, bliss and equanimity descend into him, he experiences a great inner happiness. But these experiences are not always possible in the initial stages of sadhana and do not occur every day. They happen only occasionally, with long intervals in-between. For the rest of the time, various mechanical thoughts disturb the sadhak and all kinds of difficulties arise through the actions of the adverse forces whenever they have the opportunity to attack him. Such disturbances continue until he has made much progress in his sadhana.

A sadhak who has no intensity in his sadhana will initially be unable to maintain a constant attitude of surrender and aspiration. At that time, the only support in his sadhana is to do work as service for the Mother. Without the descent of peace and bliss, life and sadhana appear dry and uninteresting. Depression, doubt and despair try to draw the sadhak away from the path of yoga. But by repeating the Mother's name, *Ma*, the sadhak can remain conscious from the very beginning with relative ease. Although *Ma*-nama-japa is quite easy to do, it is very powerful and effective. Regardless of whether or not a sadhak is practising his sadhana intensively, he may still practise the repetition of the Mother's name from the very outset; the only thing necessary for this is a firm determination.

If the sadhak practises nama-japa, faith and reliance on it will automatically come to him, even if his faith and interest in it were not very strong in the beginning. Since there is no difference between the Mother and her name, the Mother's presence always stays with the sadhak if he does nama-japa.

Also, by doing nama-japa constantly, the difficult task of remaining always conscious becomes very simple and easy, and if one remains conscious, then surrender and aspiration also gradually become easy; the sadhak develops a spontaneous faith in the presence of the Mother. While practising nama-japa it is not difficult to maintain the idea, "*I have taken refuge in you*", or the idea, "*I am your child.*" Depending upon the sadhak's nature and inclination, he can hold on to either of these thoughts or else he can aspire for the awakening of his psychic being\*. If one can always do nama-japa in this way, then surrender becomes spontaneous and easy.

If, in the initial stages of his sadhana, the sadhak does not repeat the Mother's name as described above, but simply does work for the Mother, his work does become divine work, since he has already accepted the aim of realising the Divine in a transformed mind, life and body; but this will not be very fruitful since the sadhak will not be able to remain conscious and therefore will be unable to make a conscious surrender. Indeed, it may take many years before he can remain conscious during his work and surrender consciously. On the other hand, the japa of *Ma* brings forth consciousness quickly and makes surrender easy, and when in this way the consciousness and the attitude of surrender become firm, the sadhak can become aware of the transforming work of the Divine Force during meditation and at other times.

---

\*   See Glossary.

Some people say that nama-japa has no effect when done mechanically, but if this were so, then mechanical thoughts would likewise have no effect, whereas in fact spiritual seekers have always feared mechanical thoughts and have applied innumerable methods of sadhana to stop them. For when mechanical thoughts are stopped, the sadhana comes to a point where no more personal effort is required. All paths of sadhana which aim at the realisation of the Divine make an effort to stop mechanical thoughts and concentrate the mind. Even in ordinary life, man fears mechanical thoughts and suffers from unhappiness and restlessness on account of them. If these useless mechanical thoughts have such influence, then will the name of the Divine, which is the same as the presence of the particular form of the Divine that is being evoked, have no influence at all? Scriptures such as the Vedas, Upanishads and Puranas, as well as the saints, sages, acharyas, great souls, rishis and munis, have all highly and repeatedly praised the effect of nama-japa. Thus Tulsidasji* said: *"Who am I to describe the effect of nama-japa when Rama\*\* himself is not able to explain the power of his name?"*

Mechanical thoughts come spontaneously, they do not require any effort on our part; on the contrary, for life after life, sadhana is required in order to stop them. Try to do nama-japa – let's see how easily you can do it! In fact, you will find that a firm determination and strong will are

---

\*   A famous saint and poet of northern India.
\*\*  Rama was one of the incarnations of the Divine on earth and the central character in the famous Hindu epic, the *Ramayana*.

needed for *Ma*-nama-japa. How can this japa be mechanical when it requires such a strong will and determination? It was previously said that nama-japa is easy. The reason for this is that nama-japa is easy in comparison to other methods of yoga, although at the same time it is very powerful.

# Nama-Japa in Work

The aim of Sri Aurobindo's Yoga is the transformation of the sadhak's mind, life and body into their true divine forms and the realisation of the Divine in a transformed mind, vital and body.

Work is always done with the body, while the energy behind work comes from the vital. The methods and skills that are employed in doing work come from the mind. Work is thus accomplished by the combination of these three parts of the being, the mind, the vital and the body, and since in the Yoga of Sri Aurobindo the mind, vital and body are to be transformed, the work done by them cannot be excluded from the sadhana. All necessary work should be done as sadhana, as perfectly as possible, and should be offered to the Mother with an attitude of service to her. Work done with this attitude becomes divine work. However, the sadhak can only have such an attitude when he remains always in a higher consciousness above the mind.

In the early stages of sadhana it is not possible for most sadhaks to remain in a higher consciousness while they are working, though it may be possible during meditation. In the initial stages, a sadhak remains in the mental consciousness; but through his surrender and aspiration, and by the transforming action of the Divine Power, he will eventually be able to remain in a higher consciousness even while he is working. For many sadhaks it takes a long time, even many years, to reach such a stage. Otherwise, the sadhak's mind wanders in various worlds of thought while he is working and he cannot even remember that the work he is doing is divine work.

However, if, with a little effort, the sadhak repeats the Mother's name, *Ma*, he will be able to do the divine work right from the beginning of his sadhana and offer it at the feet of the Mother. If he remains vigilant, conscious and firmly determined, he can always do nama-japa and will not forget it even in the midst of his work. He will be able to repeat the Mother's name, either with the help of his lips or silently in his mind, while engaged in any activity. Along with the japa, he may maintain the attitude, *"I am yours, I have taken refuge in you"*, or he can hold on to the idea of surrendering his whole being to the Mother, or he can aspire for the awakening of the psychic being. If the sadhak repeats the Mother's name and works in this way, he will find interest, enthusiasm, happiness, inspiration and joy in his work.

By doing divine work with this attitude, the change of consciousness takes place easily and in less time than it would otherwise. Also, work done with this attitude brings reliance upon the Mother's Grace.

The Mother has said in her *Questions and Answers*: *"In all pursuits, intellectual or active, your one motto should be, 'Remember and Offer'."* [1]

The Mother has thus said that in doing any action, one has to *'Remember and Offer'*. Unless you remember, you cannot offer your work; by doing nama-japa of *Ma*, one can remember the Mother.

# The Mother on Japa

"*I have also come to realise that for this sadhana of the body, the mantra is essential. Sri Aurobindo gave none; he said that one should be able to do all the work without having to resort to external means. Had he reached the point where we are now, he would have seen that the purely psychological method is inadequate and that a japa is necessary, because only japa has a direct action on the body. So I had to find the method all alone, to find my mantra by myself. But now that things are ready, I have done ten years of work in a few months. That is the difficulty, it requires time . . .*

*And I repeat my mantra constantly – when I am awake and even when I sleep. I say it even when I am getting dressed, when I eat, when I work, when I speak with others; it is there, just behind in the background, all the time, all the time.*

*In fact, you can immediately see the difference between those who have a mantra and those who don't. With those who have no mantra, even if they have a strong habit of meditation or concentration, something around them remains hazy and vague. Whereas the japa imparts to those who practise it a kind of precision, a kind of solidity: an armature. They become galvanised, as it were.*"[2]

Here the Mother has clearly stated how necessary it is to do nama-japa for the transformation of the body: "*I have also come to realise that for this sadhana of the body, the mantra is essential . . . because only japa has a direct action on the body."*

The Mother has also said that she completed ten years of sadhana in just a few months: *"I have done ten years of work in a few months."*

It is essential to do nama-japa all the time. The Mother herself has described how she repeated her mantra constantly: *"And I repeat my mantra constantly – when I am awake and even when I sleep. I say it even when I am getting dressed, when I eat, when I work, when I speak with others; it is there, just behind in the background, all the time, all the time."*

The Mother has differentiated between those who do nama-japa and those who concentrate and go deep into meditation but do not practise nama-japa. She has said: *"In fact, you can immediately see the difference between those who have a mantra and those who don't. With those who have no mantra, even if they have a strong habit of meditation or concentration, something around them remains hazy and vague. Whereas the japa imparts to those who practise it a kind of precision, a kind of solidity: an armature. They become galvanised, as it were."*

From these statements by the Mother it can be seen that three-quarters of the difficulties of the great and arduous task of transformation of the body will be solved by doing nama-japa. Thus the difficult process of transformation has now become easy, and the practice of this Yoga of Transformation has become possible for everyone.

# Nama-Japa in Worldly Life

The transformation of the body is the aim of everyone's life and all are advancing towards its realisation unknowingly through their work. And yet, although this is so evident and so real, most people are not conscious of this aim of life; their psychic being is not awakened and worldly life is everything for them. If these persons begin to do nama-japa, they can obtain contentment, peace and bliss and live happily in their family lives. Their psychic being can thus be awakened and in the course of time they will advance on the path of Divine Realisation, which is the ultimate goal of life.

All categories of people, the rich, the poor, the learned, the ignorant, saints as well as sinners, are suffering from family, social and global difficulties. Some are worried about money, disputes at work and political conflicts. Others are worried about family quarrels, about the misunderstandings and differences of opinion that occur between brothers, between mothers-in-law and daughters-in-law, and between fathers and sons. Some are worried about their children's illnesses, others suffer from fear of enemies, fear of serious diseases, fear of death and, in the case of women, fear of the death of their husbands or children.

All these fears and worries make a person restless and life becomes burdensome. Those who have such anxieties and fears in great measure lose their mental balance and some, unable to bear them, even commit suicide. They live a life full of sorrows and difficulties. But if such people take the help of *Ma*-nama-japa and aspire with a firm determination to do it always, then by means of this japa, they can obtain peace and happiness and will be freed from their difficulties and obstacles.

When fears and worries arise concerning something that has happened, when there are problems which you are unable to solve, or when there is an incident which causes you anxiety, then immediately start *Ma*-nama-japa and at the same time surrender the fear, anxiety, restlessness or any other obstacle or hindrance at the feet of the Mother. In other words, along with nama-japa one should think, "*I offer this at your feet, may you transform it and solve this problem.*" If nama-japa is done with this attitude, then worry, fear, anxiety and sorrow will be dispelled, peace will be established and one will receive from within clear indications for the solution to complicated problems. Difficulties and dangers will also be overcome. There will be no discord in the house of a person who does nama-japa in this way; there will be harmony among brothers and goodwill shall prevail between mother-in-law and daughter-in-law. Such families shall be honoured in society as ideal families.

Quarrels and arguments take place due to ego and selfishness; ego and selfishness give rise to jealousy and hostility. But through the influence of nama-japa, our ego and selfishness and the adverse forces are gradually purified; they are enlightened by nama-japa. Ignorance and darkness are gradually transformed by the light of nama-japa, and through the light and power of our devotion, our petty ego and selfishness will be prevented from acting.

The name *Ma* is composed of the two Sanskrit letters म (M) and आ (A). These letters are bijas (seed-syllables). म (M) is chandra-bija*, and embodies qualities such as peace and bliss, whereas आ (A) is agni-bija, the seed-syllable for spiritual fire, which purifies. By repeating the name मा (*Ma*), ignorance as well as the results of past wrongdoings will be reduced to ashes by the effect of agni-bija. By the action of chandra-bija, the divine qualities such as bliss, peace and equanimity will manifest. Then one remains in peace and happiness and wishes for the welfare of others; in this way the home turns into a spiritual ashram.

It is only by doing nama-japa that one can live peacefully and happily at home, advancing on the path towards the goal of Divine Realisation. In the past, it was not possible for such ideal families to exist in large numbers. But now the Supramental Power is doing the work of transformation and its influence is working in the earth's atmosphere. Sadhaks who have accepted transformation as the aim of their lives are now progressing on the path of yoga. Others who have not yet taken up sadhana for the transformation of mind, life and body, but who do nama-japa simply with the aim of living a peaceful and happy family life, can now achieve this through the influence of the Supramental Force. Peace and happiness can thus be established in their families. They may form ideal families in large

---

* Chandra is the Sanskrit word for moon.

numbers, and then the suffocating indiscipline, injustice, untruthfulness and falsehood that prevail in the family, the society, the country and the world will gradually diminish. This will consequently help the progress of sadhaks who have accepted transformation as the aim of their lives. The more these sadhaks progress, the more will peace and order increase in the ideal households, in the society and in the country. Everybody therefore should do nama-japa.

# Nama-Japa Can Remove Obstacles and Dangers

It has been said that the transformation of mind, life and body is a very difficult task because man's nature and its lower movements, such as lust and anger, do not want to be transformed. As soon as the transforming Supramental Force touches the sadhak, or as soon as he advances a little on the path of yoga, a small measure of peace, light, bliss and knowledge descends from above into his mind, life and body. In reaction to this descent, the movements of the lower nature – lust, anger, greed, attachment, ego, selfishness, jealousy, envy, depression, mechanical thoughts, unwillingness to change, inertia, laziness and illness – come forward one by one or in twos or threes to resist the work of transformation. The Divine Power, however, will only touch the sadhak to the extent to which he can bear its effects and in accordance with his capacity to surrender to the Divine Mother. It will not permit all the adverse forces to attack him simultaneously.

In addition to the above, misunderstandings and differences of opinion sometimes arise through our way of dealing with others. Fear of disease, fear of death and other forms of fear attack some sadhaks and make them very disturbed and restless. At such moments the sadhak should be conscious that he is being attacked by the hostile forces and continuously repeat the Mother's name, *Ma*, maintaining the idea, "*I am yours; I surrender all these opposing forces at your feet.*" In these circumstances the name should be repeated at a very fast rate.* If the sadhak holds on to this attitude of surrender and then tries in a determined way to do this type of japa, he will succeed. While doing this japa, the lips may move but there will be no audible sound. In this way, in spite of doing japa quickly, the breathing process will not be disturbed. Mechanical thoughts cannot intervene if japa is done with an attitude of surrender. If this attitude of surrender is maintained, the Mother's Power will protect the sadhak as if he were a small child and hostile attacks will not cause him any harm. Faith and dependence on nama-japa and the Mother's Power will increase.

The attacks of the hostile forces affect the minds of sadhaks who lack perfect faith and confidence in the Mother, whose sincerity for surrender is weak, who do not do *Ma*-nama-japa continuously and who do not remain alert in the face of the attacks of lust, anger, ego and selfishness, but allow them scope. If the pressure becomes intolerable, these sadhaks lose their stability and become deeply disturbed. It then becomes very difficult for them to free themselves from these obstacles. For some, this condition becomes very dangerous. But if the sadhak remains conscious and alert, not giving room to the attacks by relying on the Mother and doing *Ma*-nama-japa, then he can easily become free from the attacks of the hostile forces. For when

---

\* This type of japa is used to control undesirable and disturbing thoughts.

a person does nama-japa, the Mother's Force helps him in a very direct manner and indicates the way in which he may free himself from the clutches of the adverse powers.

*Ma*-nama-japa has to be done continuously. Along with the repetition of the Mother's name, one has to think, "*I am yours, I surrender these adverse circumstances at your feet.*" The impact of the hostile attacks and the obstacles raised by them are reduced by japa done with this attitude and after some time the obstacles are completely transformed.

By overcoming an obstacle in this way, the sadhak's interest, love and faith in nama-japa increase, and his reliance on the Mother's Force becomes stronger. Also, the sadhak's inner strength, fearlessness, courage and patience increase. Through faith and reliance on the Mother, and by maintaining an attitude of surrender along with doing nama-japa, the obstacles and hindrances in the sadhana of transformation are greatly reduced and the sadhak will not be afraid of future obstacles. The progress in sadhana that would otherwise take many years to accomplish, can thus be made within a few months.

By maintaining an attitude of surrender along with the repetition of the Mother's name, the influence of the agni-bija in the name *Ma* will slowly burn the power of the adverse forces to ashes and gradually transform these forces. Little by little adverse thoughts will decrease, for by remaining conscious and doing nama-japa with an attitude of surrender, their passage gets blocked. When wrong thoughts, fear and anxiety are no longer present, there will be no harmful pressure on the mind of the sadhak. If this much is achieved, the sadhak obtains a strong foothold on the path of sadhana. Illnesses and other obstacles do come during the process of physical transformation, but because the hands of the Mother are always resting upon the sadhak's head and blessing him, he does not become disturbed or depressed. On the contrary, remaining more and more engrossed in nama-japa, he surrenders at the feet of the Mother.

# Questions and Answers

**Question from a sadhak:** What is the significance in the Mother's saying that Sri Aurobindo gave no mantra when he has written so much on the subject?

[The sadhak then elaborates on the question with the following comments]. The Mother says, "*Sri Aurobindo gave none*", but Sri Aurobindo has written about japa in his great epic *Savitri*, in *The Synthesis of Yoga* and in his *Letters on Yoga*. He has also stated that the mantra of this yoga is the Mother's name or the Mother's name together with his own. Here are some of the references to namajapa from the writings of Sri Aurobindo:

"*As a rule the only mantra used in this Sadhana is that of the Mother or of my name and the Mother's.*" [3]

"*Any name, any form, any symbol, any offering has been held to be sufficient if there is the consecration along with it . . . .*" [4]

"*There is, of course, a third way, the reliance on the power of the mantra or name in itself . . . .*" [5]

"*The name of the Divine is usually called in for protection, for adoration, for increase of bhakti, for the opening up of the inner consciousness, for the realisation of the Divine in that aspect. As far as it is necessary to work in the subconscious for that, the Name must be effective there.*" [6]

"*Namajapa has a great power in it.*" [7]

> *"A psychic fire within must be lit into which all is thrown with the Divine Name upon it."* [8]

> *"Usually the Mother's name has the full power in it; but in certain states of consciousness the double Name may have a special effect."* [9]

(The double name *Sri Aurobindo-Mira*)

> *"Here must the traveller of the upward way –*
> *For daring Hell's kingdoms winds the heavenly route –*
> *Pause or pass slowly through that perilous space,*
> *A prayer upon his lips and the great Name."* [10]

> *"Arousing consciousness in things inert,*
> *He imposed upon dark atom and dumb mass*
> *The diamond script of the Imperishable,*
> *Inscribed on the dim heart of fallen things*
> *A paean-song of the free Infinite*
> *And the Name, foundation of eternity . . . ."* [11]

> *"A key to a Light still kept in being's core,*
> *The sun-word of an ancient mystery's sense,*
> *Her name ran murmuring on the lips of men*
> *Exalted and sweet like an inspired verse . . ."* [12]

> *"They sang Infinity's names and deathless powers*
> *In metres that reflect the moving worlds . . . ."* [13]

Also, Sri Aurobindo gave to some sadhaks the following mantras:

> *"OM  Sri Aurobindo Mira*
> *Open my mind, my heart, my life to your Light, your Love, your Power. In all things may I see the Divine."* [14]

*"OM Anandamayi Chaitanyamayi Satyamayi Parame."*

The Mother translated this Sanskrit mantra into English as:

*"Om –
She, the Delight;
She, the Consciousness;
She, the Truth;
She, the Supreme."* [15]

**Answer:** Sri Aurobindo said: *"As a rule the only mantra used in this Sadhana is that of the Mother or of my name and the Mother's."* [16]

This is the mantra of this yoga. Apart from this, Sri Aurobindo has written about japa in various places. At the time Sri Aurobindo was writing, the sadhana was at a stage where there was no special need to do mantra-japa – that is why Sri Aurobindo did not put so much emphasis upon it.* Rather, according to the Mother, Sri Aurobindo had said that one should be able to do all the work without having to resort to external means. However, in 1959 the Mother stated: *"Had he reached the point where we are now, he would have seen that the purely psychological method is inadequate and that a japa is necessary, because only japa has a direct action on the body."* [17]

Although Sri Aurobindo had written about japa and given mantras, the power in japa to

---

* This is similar to the way in which, in the various old yogas, primary importance is given to one procedure, while other procedures, although still practised, are given secondary importance.

influence the body had not been awakened or activated, because at that time the Supramental Force had not yet descended. That is why Sri Aurobindo gave the most important place to surrender and aspiration rather than to nama-japa. This has been made clear in his book *The Mother*.

In 1950 Sri Aurobindo brought the Supramental Force down into his own body and then left his body. The Mother subsequently reached a level in the Yoga of Transformation where she gave foremost importance to japa in the sadhana, saying that it was inevitable for the physical transformation. She indicated at that time that she had discovered a simple procedure for the transformation of the body. She also said: *"So I had to find the method all alone, to find my mantra by myself."* [18]

It has been recorded that prior to this, the Mother had done nama-japa in her childhood, and the Mother herself has told us that when Sri Aurobindo was present in his body, she used to do the japa of *"My Lord"*, referring to Sri Aurobindo, whenever she faced any difficulties or obstacles. By this japa all obstacles and difficulties disappeared in a short time. But after Sri Aurobindo left his physical body, whenever she repeated this japa of *"My Lord"*, she was in effect addressing herself and for this reason she gave up this japa.

What the Mother may have wished to point out in saying that Sri Aurobindo gave no mantra, is that all that Sri Aurobindo had written on the subject of nama-japa, and the Mother's own practice of it prior to her discovery of japa as a means for physical transformation, related to nama-japa as a help in sadhana and as a method for overcoming all hindrances and obstacles. But the secrets that japa is indispensable for the physical transformation, that it acts directly on the body and that by it the sadhana of many years can be accomplished in a few months, had not been revealed at that time. Those secrets were only discovered by the Mother herself. Prior to that, the transformation of the body had not begun. How then could others have known these secrets, and why should they have felt any need to know them? The significance of the Mother's statement is to give first place to japa for the transformation of the body, rather than to surrender and aspiration alone.

**Question:** If japa was not necessary during Sri Aurobindo's lifetime, and Sri Aurobindo gave first place in sadhana to aspiration, rejection and surrender, why then did he write about japa?

**Answer:** Sri Aurobindo wrote about japa because it was to be of primary importance in the future, at the time of the transformation of the body.

Avatars of the Supreme Lord possess a dual consciousness. Whilst remaining in their Divine Consciousness, they decree all the activities that will occur in the future. But when performing actions that take place in the present, they remain in their human consciousness. Occasionally, when necessary, the avatars also do the work of the present from their Divine Consciousness, but this happens very rarely. That is why Sri Aurobindo, knowing that japa would be necessary in the future, wrote about it, but did not apply it in his own sadhana. His writing about japa was an act of his Divine Consciousness.

Avatars come as representatives of the human race in order to establish a new Truth and Ideal and therefore they do not always remain in the Divine Consciousness, but, remaining in the human consciousness, they behave as if they were human beings. This explains why during his lifetime Sri Aurobindo did not give the supreme place to japa in the sadhana. At that time the Supramental Force had not yet descended upon earth and thus the power latent in nama-japa to awaken the body consciousness, illumine the body and prepare its cells to aspire, had not yet manifested. The latent power in nama-japa was only revealed after the Supramental Force had descended.

In 1950 Sri Aurobindo brought the Supramental Power down to earth and left his body. The Mother then held the Supramental Force in her own body and carried out the work of physical transformation. She subsequently reached a stage in the process of the transformation of the body where she realised that japa was absolutely indispensable, and she was able to accomplish ten years of sadhana in a few months.

**Question:** This is difficult to understand. Did Sri Aurobindo not reach the stage in sadhana at which the Mother had arrived?

**Answer:** Sri Aurobindo did not reach the stage of transformation which the Mother reached, for during Sri Aurobindo's lifetime the Supramental Power had not yet descended upon earth and was not doing the work of physical transformation. The transformation of the body was not possible without the Supramental Force. Sri Aurobindo brought the Supramental Force down to earth and sacrificed his body. After that, the Supramental Force started the work of physical transformation through the Mother. Sri Aurobindo found that the adharas of the sadhaks were not prepared to hold the Supramental Force, in a similar way to that in which the earth was not able to hold the force of the descent of the river Ganga; and like Lord Shiva receiving the first impact of the descent of Ganga, Sri Aurobindo brought the Supramental Force down into his own body and sacrificed it.* Holding the Supramental Force in her body, the Mother started the work of transformation. After leaving his physical body, Sri Aurobindo remained in his subtle body helping the Mother with this work. This is the explanation of why Sri Aurobindo did not reach the stage of physical transformation which the Mother had reached by working with the Supramental Force.

Sri Aurobindo and the Mother are avatars of the Divine Sachchidananda. An avatar takes on a human body and, as a representative of humanity, does the work of showing the right path to mankind. He does not do all works applying his Divine Power. All Divine Qualities and Powers are

---

\* Bhagiratha, an ancient king of the solar dynasty, practised austerities to bring the Goddess Ganga (river Ganga) down to the earth in order to restore to life the thousands of princes of his dynasty who had been burnt to ashes, due to the curse of a rishi. Lord Shiva, who was very much pleased with Bhagiratha's austerities, agreed to receive the initial impact of the force of the descent of the Goddess Ganga on his own head in order to save the earth from destruction.

constantly present in the avatar, but because he comes as the representative of humanity, he refrains from applying his Divine Force in establishing the Ideal for which he has incarnated.

Sri Aurobindo incarnated as an avatar in order to be the representative of the human race, and therefore, doing the work of the present while remaining in his human consciousness, he did not stress the importance of nama-japa for physical transformation, which would only take place in the future. But for the stage of body-transformation at which the Mother had arrived, surrender and aspiration alone were insufficient. The Mother found nama-japa to be indispensable for the transformation of the body. The Mother said: *"I have done ten years of work in a few months."*

**Question:** The Mother herself did japa with various mantras and spoke about them. Which mantra then should we repeat?

**Answer:** We will repeat only the Mother's name, *Ma*. This single syllable, *Ma*, is the mantra. Sri Aurobindo has said that in this Integral Yoga the mantra is *"that of the Mother or of my name and the Mother's."*

The Mother herself did japa with different mantras at different times. While she was doing nama-japa, the sadhaks of the Ashram, or anyone else who came to the samadhi at that time, could hear the japa of the Mother. The Mother used to repeat aloud the mantra – *Om Namo Bhagavate Sri Aravindaya*.

In the schools of the old yogas there are various mantras, but only the name is repeated at all times. There are different types of mantra, such as the Sri Rama and Sri Krishna mantras, but while mantras are repeated for a limited period of time only, nama-japa is done at all times. The Mother told some sadhaks to repeat the name, *Ma*, and some others to repeat the mantra, *Om Namo Bhagavate*. The Mother herself repeated this mantra for a long time.

The transformation is being done by the Supramental Force. The Supramental Force and the Mother are one and the same Truth. Therefore, when one surrenders to the Mother, the Supramental Power starts working. In *Letters on Yoga* and many other books, Sri Aurobindo told us to surrender to the Mother. At several places in *The Mother*, Sri Aurobindo very clearly stated that one has to surrender only to the Mother. The Mother is the dynamic Force of the Divine; the Mother's Power and the Divine are one and inseparable. When something is surrendered to the Mother, it means that it is automatically surrendered to the Divine. Since the Mother's name is the mantra of this yoga, this is the name we should repeat.

The Mother repeated many mantras and also put many mantras into writing. A sadhak can repeat any mantra that has come from the Mother. All these mantras have an influence on the body, but since the name, *Ma*, is only one syllable, it is very easy to repeat. Even when the Mother's Force starts the work of transformation in the sadhak's body, it is easy to repeat the name, *Ma*, without moving the lips, in that particular place in the body where the Mother's Force is working.

Since the Mother did not wish to repeat her own name, she repeated the name of the Divine. But for us this does not apply; for us it is correct to repeat the Mother's name. Since the Mother is the dynamic Force of the Lord Sri Aurobindo, we surrender to her for the transformation of our mind, vital and body. To repeat her name is logical, immediately effective and in accordance with the shastras.

**Question:** In Sri Aurobindo's book *The Mother* we have been instructed to surrender to the Divine Shakti. When asked by one of the sadhaks of the Ashram whether the Mother of the Ashram was the incarnation of the Divine Shakti, Sri Aurobindo replied "*Yes.*" Sri Aurobindo also made the statement that the Mother of the Ashram is the Adya Bhagavati Shakti (the Supreme Mother). Whatever Sri Aurobindo has said is the truth, but then, if the Mother is the incarnation of the Supreme Mother, why did she not know beforehand that japa was inevitable for the transformation of the body? Why did she discover this only after the physical transformation had begun? This is difficult to understand.

**Answer:** Since we are only human beings, it is naturally difficult for us to understand this.

The incarnations of the Divine always possess the Divine Consciousness and Power as well as the human consciousness. Since the avatar is the representative of humanity, he works from the human consciousness, but the moment he wishes to act from his Divine Consciousness he can do so, as was the case with Sri Aurobindo. Unless it is unavoidable, the avatars do not use their Divine Power; they behave like human beings so that men will not be able to perceive their divinity. The reason for this is that it is only if the avatar works from his human consciousness that men will be able to accept his Ideal. That is why Sri Aurobindo and the Mother did sadhana as if they were human beings and had to face every kind of obstacle and hindrance.

In the initial stages of sadhana, japa was not so necessary, but at the time of the transformation of the body it became so. The Mother realised this and spoke about it.

It is very difficult for the human mind to understand the conduct of the avatar. For example, during the battle described in the *Mahabharata*, Sri Krishna, despite his omniscience, used to consult Sahadeva* whenever he wished to know anything about the future or about any secret matter.

**Question:** Nama-japa was practised in all the former yogas but no one achieved the transformation of the body. What then is the secret behind the Mother's statement that in this Yoga of Transformation, japa is inevitable? Would you kindly explain this?

**Answer:** In the old yogas transformation was not the aim; the time for that had not yet arrived. The transforming Supramental Power had not been

---
\* Sahadeva possessed an inherent capacity to know the future.

established on earth and therefore the Power latent in the Divine Name for transforming the body had not yet manifested. Nama-japa was not being done in order to realise the aim of transformation. Indeed, no one was even conscious of this aim – the transformation of the mind, vital and body into their Divine Principles which will completely free a person from pain, suffering, disease, old age and death. Since the time for the realisation of this aim had not yet arrived, the incarnations of the Divine and the great souls did not descend to earth for that purpose. They came only to accelerate the process of evolution that would make the future goal of transformation possible. This they accomplished. But once the hour for physical transformation had arrived, the Mother and Sri Aurobindo came down to establish the Supramental Power on earth. Due to the establishment of the Supramental Force, the power inherent in nama-japa is now working directly on the body. The Mother herself realised this. Thus, by doing japa, the arduous work of physical transformation has become easy. Therefore, if we accept this aim and constantly repeat the Mother's name, *Ma*, with an attitude of surrender, the realisation of this aim of transformation will be comparatively easy and we will be protected from obstacles and hindrances.

**Question:** The Mother has said that a person may either receive his mantra through an inner inspiration, or he may spontaneously hear from within a mantra that is appropriate for him. This is not possible for beginners, so which name should we repeat?

**Answer:** The mantra or name that should be repeated is one that has been given by Sri Aurobindo or the Mother. Sri Aurobindo has said:

> "As a rule the only mantra used in this Sadhana is that of the Mother or of my name and the Mother's." [19]

Sri Aurobindo has also given the mantra:

> Om Anandamayi Chaitanyamayi Satyamayi Parame *

The Mother has given the following mantras:

> Sri Aravindah Sharanam Mama
> (Sri Aurobindo is my refuge)
>
> Om
>
> Om Namo Bhagavate **
>
> Om Namo Bhagavate Sri Aravindaya
>
> Namami Sri Matrimiraravindau
> (I bow to Mother Mira and Sri Aurobindo)
>
> Sri Matrimiraravindau Sharanam Mama
> (Mother Mira and Sri Aurobindo are my refuge)
>
> Vijayetam Sri Matrimiraravindau
> (Victory to Mother Mira and Sri Aurobindo)

---

\* See page 24.
\*\* The Mother's interpretation of this mantra:
"OM NAMO BHAGAVATE.
These three words. For me they meant:
OM – I implore the Supreme Lord.
NAMO – Obeisance to Him.
BHAGAVATE – Make me divine." [20]

Out of the above, a sadhak can do the japa of any name or mantra to which he feels spontaneously inclined. All of these mantras and names have extraordinary power and influence, and whichever one is repeated will have an effect upon the body. But in this Integral Yoga we are surrendering to the Mother and the name *Ma*, which consists of only one syllable, is easy to repeat. One may also regularly repeat for some time during the day: *Om Namo Bhagavate* and *Sri Aravindah Sharanam Mama*. For the rest of the time, one can repeat the Mother's name, *Ma*, or one can repeat the name which has come from within.

# Obstacles and Hindrances

Everyone in this world desires peace and happiness. But due to opposing negative qualities such as lust, anger, greed, delusion, ego, selfishness, disappointment, hopelessness, violence and ill will, which lie inherent within us, we cannot obtain the happiness and peace we wish for. These negative qualities are the great adversaries on the path towards the realisation of the Divine. Among them, lust, anger, ego and selfishness are the most powerful. If the sadhak becomes aware of the workings of these four great enemies and surrenders them at the feet of the Mother, he can then easily surrender the others as well.

The sadhak can easily recognise sex and anger and their movements, but it is not easy for him to recognise his ego and selfishness. We shall discuss the workings of these opposing forces one by one.

## Anger

Anger is present in the nature of the vital and is extremely powerful; it immediately overpowers the buddhi\*. Sometimes it attacks an individual directly, sometimes it attacks through another person and sometimes it derives its support from an event.

When the Divine Power starts its work of transformation in the spiritual seeker, it touches

---
\* Intellect or power of discrimination.

all the defects and imperfections of his mind and vital in order to transform them. Like a snake that raises its hood furiously when its tail is beaten with a stick, all the imperfections lying dormant in the lower nature rise up and obstruct the Divine Power's work of transformation. If the sadhak is not conscious at that time, then the nature and qualities of others will appear to him to be at fault and he will always believe that it is others alone that are in the wrong. He will be under the delusion that others are behaving badly towards him and he in turn will behave antagonistically towards them, to such a degree that even trifles become the cause of controversies and quarrels. When those sadhaks who have a strong temper are attacked by anger, their hearts burn with it and until they throw these vibrations of anger out towards another person, they feel abnormally restless and agitated. When they get angry with someone, they either insult him or quarrel with him, or even come to blows. After the incident has passed, the anger is appeased and, if the mind has not been enlightened very much by the soul, the sadhak will think, *"What I have done was perhaps not right, but the anger, restlessness, uneasiness and agitation that were burning in my heart would not have gone if I had not expressed my anger."*

In sadhana, it is a mistake to justify and support this unhelpful conduct. Anger does not become weakened in this way; it gets stronger and returns with greater force during the next attack. This is contrary to the methods of self-control and transformation.

One method of transformation is to understand that it is irrelevant whether others behave well or badly. The sadhak should think, *"Anger itself is a hostile force, so I should never give scope to it."* Thinking in this way and remembering the name of the Mother, he should surrender the anger that is churning inside him at her feet. It is obvious that at such times one cannot concentrate or sit quietly; but still one should call the Mother and pray to her and think, *"By the Force of the Mother, this anger will definitely be transformed and since I am the Mother's child, she will certainly protect me."* At such times, the name of the Mother should be repeated at a very fast rate. The first time one practises this, it may take quite some time before the anger subsides; but if the sadhak succeeds once, then this will increase his courage, patience and confidence for the next occasion. The second time, his concentration on the Mother's name will be easier than the first time. If the name is repeated very fast, anger will go away comparatively quickly.

One may also adopt the following method: when anger arises, do not act on it, but consult someone who can give proper advice. If that person is able to advise you well, the anger will quickly vanish and concentration, faith in the Mother and the attitude of surrender will increase. The agitation of the sadhak will be dispelled and he will be able to feel peace and ananda and the presence of the Mother.

It is not at all the right thing to express the attack of any adverse force in action, for in this way the attacks of these forces increase and gain in strength. Ninety-nine times out of a hundred, decisions taken in anger will be wrong; their outcome will be very bad. As long as the anger has not subsided, one should not attempt to solve any problem.

## Lust

Lust and anger are both very powerful, but the movements of lust are more difficult to recognise than those of anger. Anybody can easily identify anger, but it is more difficult to recognise the attacks of lust.

When the desire for sex is active or predominant in a sadhak, if he has not made a firm decision to be free from it and to transform it, and if there is any insincerity in his will to surrender at the feet of the Mother, then a friendship will develop towards someone of the opposite sex. In the early stages, this friendship does not appear to be wrong; the individual imagines that it is a pure relationship. But if there is a longing to meet and talk again and again and if without this contact one feels restless, then it is not at all a pure relationship. In this case it is undoubtedly a sexual impulse from the vital plane coming in disguise, and if the sadhak is not cautious, it will open the way to a fall. These are the tactics adopted by the desire for sex, which arises from within.

In a psychic relationship a person wishes for the welfare of the other and gives help when necessary, but he does not become anxious or restless when he is not able to meet or talk with the other person.

Whether a relation between opposite sexes is pure or not, a sadhak should always remain cautious, right from the beginning. He should maintain only as much contact and conversation as is necessary for the work. If the sadhak is not careful from the beginning, in many cases a relationship will eventually become impure.

Those who have sincerely taken refuge in the Mother are protected by her at every step; she does not allow the sadhak to slip from the path easily. Indications from the Mother and obstacles and hindrances come again and again in order to make him conscious; but if he fails to become so, he will fall into the clutches of desire. Yet even in that state, the Mother's Power will continue to help him to become conscious. The Mother will certainly protect the sadhak if he becomes conscious, remembers her name and calls her with sincere ardour from the core of his heart. However, at this stage, it will be very difficult for him to do this. If the sadhak does not care for the Mother's protection and does not follow the spiritual path with a strong central conviction, then he may return to the ordinary life. But if the sadhak has once sincerely taken refuge in the Divine and has accepted this path of spirituality, and then afterwards returns to the worldly life, the Divine will not entirely forsake him. The sadhak will suffer much from sorrow and difficulties in his family life. Then, either in this life or the next, he will again return to the spiritual path; the spiritual progress that has been achieved in this life will not be lost.

Those sadhaks who have a strong central surrender, unmixed with desires and attachments, and who have taken refuge in the Mother like a small child, will also be attacked by lust and anger and other movements of the lower nature. Because, until the body is transformed, all the opposing forces, such as lust, anger, ego and selfishness, remain within it. Moreover, when the Divine Power begins the work of transformation, it touches these movements of the lower nature in order to transform them. As soon as they are touched by the Divine Power, they immediately come to the front to obstruct the Mother's work. To the extent that the sadhak is able to bear it, the Divine Power allows the lower nature to come forward for transformation. In truth, the obstacles and hindrances created by the adverse forces actually help the sadhak to progress in his sadhana. If the sadhak remains conscious and under the protection of the Mother's Power and does not encourage the attacks of the adverse forces, but surrenders them at her feet and repeats her name, then she will certainly protect him. The Mother is always waiting to save the sadhak and her Power protects him as soon as his surrender becomes free from pretence, is straightforward and without desire and attachment.

## Ego and Selfishness

Ego and selfishness are very close friends; one cannot remain without the other. Ego is one with the body; a person with a name and form is in himself ego. Therefore ego will remain in the body as long as the body is not transformed. Those yogis and rishis who remain constantly in the Brahmic Consciousness, having separated themselves from their mind, vital and body, may, if they return to the physical consciousness, be attacked by such enemies as ego, selfishness, lust and anger, should these be given the opportunity.

In general, the opposing movements of lust, anger, greed, attachment, ego and selfishness, are not equally strong in each individual; usually one of them predominates. In some lust is the strongest, in some anger and in others greed and attachment. In a person in whom ego and selfishness are very strong, lust and anger may be less active or even dormant. But this is not a universal rule; in some cases, all the opposing movements may be strong.

Generally, those who do service to uplift their country – powerful and influential leaders, skilful, dedicated and competent doctors, famous physical scientists and expert engineers – may all possess ego to a very high degree, whereas lust, anger and other negative movements in the lower nature may not be active in them. None of these persons are conscious of their ego, for an individual can become aware of his ego only if he lives in the inner spiritual consciousness. The ego is so well disguised that, with the help of the mind alone, it is not possible to understand it or see through its deceptive ways.

It is absolutely necessary for sadhaks of Sri Aurobindo's Yoga of Transformation to become conscious of their ego, for it has to be transformed. The sadhak cannot surrender his ego if he is not conscious of it. The hostile forces create many kinds of obstacles and hindrances on our path, and without surrender, the Divine Supramental Power will not do the work of transformation. In other words, if the sadhak is not conscious of his ego, he will not be able to progress in sadhana. The easiest way for him to become conscious of it, is to completely surrender at the feet of the Mother and remember her name, *Ma*, as soon as he enters the path of this yoga. This indicates the central resolve to surrender.

When the psychic being awakens, a person feels impelled to begin sadhana for the realisation of the Divine. Depending upon the choice of his psychic being, the sadhak will either do sadhana while remaining in family life or else he will renounce it. But without the awakening of his psychic being, he cannot have a firm determination to realise the Divine. The psychic being awakens in the individual either in the natural course of evolution or by the Divine Grace. It may also awaken when the person comes into contact with sadhaks and spiritual organisations or when he reads spiritual texts.

The psychic being is the Divine's own form, the true Eternal Being. Its nature is supreme Bliss, supreme Peace, supreme Knowledge, supreme Equanimity and supreme Kindness and Compassion. The psychic being exists in man in order to manifest the Divine in the mind, the vital and the physical body. As soon as it awakens, the individual makes a central resolve to realise the Divine and begins to do sadhana. But the psychic being does not always remain in front. Until the sadhak reaches the goal, ego, selfishness, desire and the attachments of the mind and vital rise up in the course of sadhana to be transformed and repeatedly cover the psychic being. Some sadhaks consciously make the central resolve to realise the Divine and simultaneously make the central resolve to surrender their entire being at the feet of the Mother. Other sadhaks, however, make a central resolve to realise the Divine and start sadhana, but are not conscious of the necessity of surrendering their entire being. After progressing a little, they become conscious of this necessity and make the central resolve to surrender completely, consecrating their mind, vital and body and offering them at the feet of the Divine. At that time, the movements of the lower nature – ego, selfishness, lust, anger, greed, desire, pride and envy – are still present in their mind, vital and body. The will and determination not to act upon one's desires and passions and the resolution to surrender them at the feet of the Mother is called central surrender.

In some sadhaks the psychic being awakens and they accept the spiritual path in order to realise the Divine; but due to a lack of intensity in their aspiration, they cannot remain conscious of their central resolve and their will to surrender. When these sadhaks progress further on the path of sadhana, then they too, after a longer or shorter period of time, will again become conscious of their central resolve and will surrender in order to realise the Divine.

The lower nature remains present in all sadhaks, whether they are conscious of their central resolve and surrender right from the beginning or whether they become so only after some time. Those whose central resolve and surrender are not mixed with desires and passions can be sure from the outset of reaching the goal. Those whose central resolve and surrender are mixed with passions and desires – such as becoming a great sadhak or achieving name and fame or acquiring power – will face obstacles and hindrances in their sadhana which may purify their central resolve and surrender; otherwise these sadhaks may nourish their passions and desires and then forsake their aim of realizing the Divine and return to the ordinary life for a few or even many years. While in ordinary life, they undergo much suffering and restlessness and all kinds of struggles. Life becomes unbearable; it becomes miserable with sorrow and suffering in a way that may be likened to the life of a moth that continuously scorches itself in the flame of a lamp. Although they suffer terribly from these torments, they are unable to become free from them. However, if at that time they call the Mother intensely from the core of their hearts, asking her to save them, and if they surrender completely, relying on her with faith, then they will be saved from their condition and return to the path of spirituality. Otherwise, the present lives of those sadhaks will end in pain and sorrow.

Those whose central aim and surrender are not mixed with desires and passions will also face obstacles and hindrances at the time of the transformation of their mind, vital and body; but since they are able to remain conscious, they will surrender everything at the feet of the Mother. The Power of the Mother will always help the sadhaks on the way towards their goal, protecting them from, or carrying them through, all kinds of obstacles and hindrances.

# Harmony in Collective Work

It has already been explained that once the sadhak surrenders, the Supramental Force will transform his mind, life and body into Divine Truth. The sadhak will then become completely free from sorrow, suffering, ignorance, old age, sickness and death. He will be guided by the Supramental Power.

Those who have become transformed in this way will be called Supramental Beings. Just as in the process of evolution, the animals have continued to exist after the advent of man, so human beings will continue to exist after the Supramental race has been established.

Since the Supramental Consciousness and the Supramental race will be established on earth through this yoga, the transformation of the Universal Nature is inevitable. Since it is the transformation of the Universal Nature that is to take place, the sadhana of this yoga is not individual but collective. This is why the goal of transformation cannot be realised by the sadhana of a single individual. A large number of sadhaks are required. Study groups, student societies, meditation centres and integral schools will be the means for spreading this yoga. Sadhaks will come together in these places to do work as sadhana and surrender it at the feet of the Mother. In this yoga, establishing these organisations and doing collective work within them is an indispensable sadhana for the attainment of the goal.

Harmony should be maintained during collective work, despite the fact that sadhaks have different natures. If a sadhak can achieve harmony with others right from the beginning of his sadhana, then by this relatively simple means he will be able to control his 'elephant-like ego', in a way similar to that in which an elephant handler is able to control this huge animal using only a small iron hook. By the Grace of the Divine Mother, the arduous sadhana of transformation will become very easy for him. But since we have not understood this secret, we clash with one another and create mountain-like obstacles that stand in the way of our own progress. If, however, a sadhak makes the firm resolve to surrender at the feet of the Mother as soon as he enters the path of sadhana, and repeats her name, he will then be able to understand this secret by her Grace, and he will not quarrel but will remain calm and quiet and continue with his sadhana under any kind of adverse circumstance.

# Causes of Disharmony

When the sadhak first begins his sadhana, his mind, vital and body and their inherent lower qualities, such as ego, selfishness, lust, anger, greed and attachment are not transformed. Complete transformation takes many years. At the beginning of his sadhana the sadhak lives in the mental consciousness, which is full of imperfections and defects. The mental consciousness is very limited and, since it does not have complete and perfect knowledge, each person has a different nature and a different angle of vision. Each individual will perceive the same thing differently according to his own consciousness; and following his own ideas and opinions, he will believe that he is right and others are wrong. It is due to these differences in opinion and judgment that we cannot maintain harmony with one another.

A further cause of disharmony is that a person who lives in the mental consciousness decides what is right or wrong, just or unjust, according to the standards of morality. He cannot understand correctly what is true and what is false, what is just and what is unjust from the viewpoint of Truth. He is not able to deal with another person according to that person's particular nature, nor is he able to maintain harmony. Those works that establish harmony and uplift life are in reality true and just works, even if they appear unjust from the social and moral point of view, while actions and behaviour that create divisions and become obstacles on the path of spiritual progress are unjust. But the sadhak cannot understand this secret unless he possesses the spiritual Truth-Consciousness. This is why conflicts arise in families, society and the world in general as well as in spiritual organisations. On the spiritual path, the way remains open for controversies to arise until the sadhak has gone beyond the mental consciousness and judges each situation, thing and event from the spiritual point of view.

At the beginning of his sadhana, the sadhak does not have spiritual vision, nor is he able to take decisions from a higher consciousness. He begins his sadhana and does collective work with imperfections and defects such as ego, selfishness, lust, anger, greed, ignorance, jealousy and revolt present in his nature. But if he surrenders at the feet of the Mother like a small child and repeats her name, *Ma*, with firm determination from the outset, his mind will be illumined by her Grace and by the power of her name. He will then understand that doing the Mother's work is his sadhana. By doing work for the Mother, the effect of the Supramental Force will spread in the world and many people will become conscious of the transforming Supramental Power and accept this yoga. By the action of the Supramental Force working through the sadhaks, the dark forces in the world will gradually be transformed. This is because the mind, vital and body of the sadhak come from the Universal Nature and remain linked with it. The powers of the adverse forces, such as ignorance, darkness and injustice, will decline in proportion to the number of people who take refuge in the Supramental Shakti; the obstacles and hindrances in sadhana will diminish in proportion to the decrease in the power of the adverse forces in the world.

For this reason it is absolutely necessary to establish study circles, create centres for sadhana and integral education and spread the ideal of the Mother and Sri Aurobindo. When the sadhak understands this secret, he will give the highest priority to these works in his sadhana in order to realise the aim. He will look upon himself as a servant, an instrument or a dependent of the Mother and he will remain on guard against the activities of ego and selfishness.

If the sadhak works with this mental attitude and surrenders at the feet of the Mother, he will be able to go beyond the mental consciousness and reach a higher consciousness. Then, instead of considering situations, events and objects from the mental-moral standpoint, he will see them from a spiritual point of view.

The spiritual approach and the way of action of the consciousness that is above the mind are as follows:

A sadhak should not act against a person who insults or opposes him if he finds rising within him reactions of anger, jealousy, enmity and envy, for this will cause hindrances and obstacles in the work of the Mother's organisations. In such cases it is better to tolerate the person who is creating the difficulty than to oppose him.

Similarly, if any situation, event or work is considered unjust or wrong from the moral standpoint and if by opposing it obstacles are generated that hinder the Mother's work and give rise within to ego, selfishness, anger, envy, jealousy, enmity or resistance, in other words the movements of the dark forces, then in such situations the sadhak should not offer any opposition, because opposition will not remove the difficulty.

A person who does good works in the world, benefiting society and the country, will have to face obstacles and hindrances. He will not only enjoy prestige and appreciation, but will also have to face humiliation and defamation. The race of Supramental Beings united with the Supramental Consciousness will be established in this death-bound world and the earth will be transformed into a Divine Heaven. Suffering, pain, injustice, untruth and falsehood will all be dispelled. The sadhaks who take part in implementing this great undertaking and work for the spreading of this Truth will likewise not be able to escape facing obstacles and hindrances, as well as prestige and humiliation. They will advance towards the goal by keeping the aim in front, without caring about either pain and sorrow or honour and dishonour. They will surrender these at the feet of the Mother and remain under her protection. It is one's ego that becomes affected by honour and dishonour, and the ego is a great obstacle in sadhana and in works done for the Mother as sadhana. Therefore, to overcome honour and dishonour means to overcome ego. If one can do this, it is a great progress in sadhana.

Those who do the Mother's work under the influence of ego and selfishness, with the aim of acquiring name and fame, will try to do only such works as will bring them the name and fame they seek and they will act against anything that stands in the way of their purpose. Obstacles are thereby created which hinder the Mother's work. But such sadhaks do not in fact obtain what they seek. If name and fame are sought after, they cannot be caught, just as a person cannot catch his own shadow. But if a person does not seek name and fame, then, just like his shadow, name and fame will run behind him.

The desire for name and fame is hidden within some sadhaks from the beginning of their sadhana. But if they have firm faith and dependence on the Mother, they will be able to see through the hidden forms under which ego and selfishness are working, and in spite of having the desire for name and fame and power within them, they will not translate this desire into action. This means that they will refrain from pursuing any crooked or devious means to acquire name, fame, power and position.

# The Mother's Inspiration from Within

Those who have joined the Mother's organisations but do not have a sincere attitude, and those who have remained outside the centres and have not accepted the Mother's work as their sadhana or given it the highest place in their lives, may apply devious means to bring an organisation under their control in order to satisfy their ego, their drive for power and position and their selfish interests. If they cannot satisfy their self-interest and ego through the work given to them, they do not hesitate to harm or destroy the organisation. One has to deal with such persons according to the situation. The best method is to receive the Mother's inspiration from within and act accordingly. When faced with such a difficult situation, if a sadhak aspires intensely with firm faith and confidence to receive the Mother's inspiration from within, he will certainly get it. This inspiration will come despite the presence within him of ego, lust, anger and other defects, provided he does not put these defects into action but aspires to surrender them at the feet of the Mother. The more intense his aspiration and call, the sooner the inspiration will come to him. But even when the intensity of his aspiration is not very strong, if he seeks inspiration from the Mother and waits for it, sooner or later he will receive it. He should always act according to this inspiration. When faced with a difficult situation one should not entertain any other thoughts or seek help from any other source; for if, in order to achieve success in your work, you are guided by the judgments of your own mind or if you take the advice of others, this will obstruct the Mother's inspiration from within. The inspiration that comes from within is unmistakable; one does not doubt whether it has come from some other force.

If ego and selfishness are active in a sadhak, then he may get a false inspiration coming from an adverse force disguised in the form of the Mother. But if he takes refuge at her feet like a small child and repeats her name, *Ma*, the suggestions of the adverse forces will not come, or if they do, he can clearly recognise them for what they really are.

In the practice of this arduous Yoga of Transformation, the safest and least difficult path is to surrender completely at the feet of the Mother. We have to do our allotted work for her with the utmost sincerity and with complete dependence upon her. We have to do nama-japa continuously. If we do this much, then the Mother will always save her organisations. She helps the sadhak to reach his goal, protecting him from all kinds of obstacles and hindrances and the terrible attacks of the adverse forces.

# Attacks from the Hostile Forces in the Process of Transformation

Some sadhaks have intense aspiration right from the beginning of their sadhana; their psychic being awakens and they experience great joy. But after some time has passed in this condition, the Divine Power descends into the adhara (mind-vital-body) and touches the dormant impure parts of the mind and vital in order to transform them. When they receive this touch, jealousy, envy, hatred, hostility, lust, anger, greed, attachment, depression, despair, inertia, etc., come forward one by one in order to prevent the transformation and they stand as a veil between the psychic being and the mind and vital. The adverse forces use these negative movements as their instruments, sometimes attacking the sadhak from within, sometimes from without, through a person or an event. If the sadhak is not conscious, he will not recognise the adverse attack for what it is and he will react against it by blaming the person or the event. In other words, he will try to resolve the matter by external measures, convinced that it is the person or the event that is the cause of all the difficulties. He thinks, *"Such and such a person has done me an injustice,"* and he then wants to solve the problem through external means. For example, he may think, *"It will be safer if I leave this place where such things are happening."* But as long as the sadhak holds on to such ideas and thinks of resorting to such external measures, the attacks of the adverse forces will continue to increase. If the sadhak does not become conscious, the adverse forces may even drag him away from the path of sadhana, at least for some time.

If the mind of the sadhak is enlightened by the Divine Power or by the psychic being, he will not imagine a person or a place to be the cause of the difficulties he is facing. He will understand these situations clearly and will be able to tell himself, *"Because my mind, vital and body are weak, they are giving scope to all these attacks."* If for example someone speaks roughly or badly to him, with or without justification, it will not create turmoil within him if his vital is strong and pure. He will realise that, *"The Divine Power did not prevent these outer attacks because they have taken place in order to transform the parts of me that are weak."* Thus remaining calm and quiet, he will try to prevent reactions from taking place within himself and he will surrender the unpurified parts of his being at the feet of the Mother. If he acts in this manner, the attacks of the adverse forces will decrease in strength and the sadhak's faith in and dependence on the Power of the Mother will increase. He will then surrender with enthusiasm. Such an awakening in sadhana takes a long time to develop, but if the name, *Ma*, is repeated always, the sadhak's mind, vital and body become purified comparatively quickly and his psychic being awakens. The Power of the Mother will then descend and start the work of transforming his mind, vital and body. When his mind is illumined by the psychic being and the Mother's Power, the sadhak will easily understand the workings of the anti-divine forces. He will then be able to transcend the stage of mental consciousness and rise above it to a higher consciousness.

The adverse forces attack the sadhak in various ways. Many kinds of disease may appear, for example, or the sadhak may misinterpret the behaviour of his friends as being that of enemies and at some other times his friends may actually become hostile towards him. During such periods, the sadhak finds darkness all around him and for a while he may feel an aversion for life and for yoga. Fear, restlessness, depression and despair cause his intellect to become confused; but if he has taken refuge in the Mother's name, *Ma*, he can remain unshaken and remember her name without being perturbed by the powerful attacks. If one remembers the Mother's name with firm faith and sincerity, then her Power will manifest itself immediately. All kinds of darkness, depression and hopelessness will then disappear, the sadhak's faith in and reliance on the Divine will increase twofold and his love and eagerness for nama-japa will intensify. He will not fear future attacks. Relying upon the Mother and keeping full faith in her, the sadhak will joyfully march forward on the path of yoga, despite the recurrence of obstacles and hindrances. Surrender and japa of the Mother's name become an impenetrable armour for the sadhak, protecting him from all sorts of obstacles and dangers from the beginning of his sadhana.

Qualities that are inherent in the nature of the mind, vital and body, such as laziness, excessive sleep, inertia, lust, anger, greed, attachment, ego, selfishness, jealousy and hostility, all become hindrances on the path for the realisation of the Divine, which is the sadhak's aim in life. These forces have been working independently, according to their own inherent nature, from the beginning of creation. Because he has developed intelligence, man controls himself in front of others on certain occasions and under certain circumstances. But most men use their intelligence as an instrument to secretly fulfil their desires. The adverse forces do not want to change their nature and do not want to fall under the control of the Higher Power, so when the sadhak advances on the path of Divine Realisation, they apply their full strength to obstruct him; they constantly try to drag the sadhak away from the spiritual path, using their powers, stratagems and devious means. When the asuric (demonic) power gets an opportunity, it uses the sadhak's own lower nature as its instrument and attacks him. Since the impurities of the lower nature are very powerful in human beings, sadhaks of the old yogas separated the soul (jivatma) from the body, mind and vital and thus achieved Mukti, Nirvana or Divine Realisation. Since they found it impossible to gain victory over the adverse forces, they left them as they were.

In the Yoga of Sri Aurobindo, the mind, vital and body and their nature and qualities will be transformed into their Divine Principles and, as a result, this death-bound world will be turned into a Divine Heaven. Although so far the hostile powers have been invincible, they will not be able to remain so before the Supramental Shakti; they will be transformed by the Supramental Power into the Divine Essence and Truth of the Supreme Lord.

But these forces do not want to be transformed, so they are ever alert and active, constantly trying to attack the sadhak in order to pull him down from the path of sadhana. The hostile forces are very cunning and much more powerful than the sadhak himself; it is impossible for the sadhak to confront them with his own strength. That is why the sadhaks of this yoga take refuge in the Power of the Mother from the beginning of their sadhana to the end and constantly repeat the Mother's name, *Ma*, surrendering entirely at her feet. The sadhana thus consists of remaining always conscious and surrendering to the Mother completely. As a result, the mind, vital and body will be transformed by the Supramental Power, that is, by the Power of the Mother. The sadhak must always be conscious and not give his consent to adverse impulses and their action upon his mind, vital and body; he should surrender them at the feet of the Divine Shakti. The Supramental Force will then do the work of transformation.

If the sadhak does not surrender, the Supramental Power will not transform him by force, but if he aspires for the Mother's Power to help him to surrender, her Power will certainly do so; indeed, it is waiting to give this help. In the second chapter of *The Mother*, Sri Aurobindo has explained: *"In Yoga also it is the Divine who is the Sadhaka and the Sadhana; it is his Shakti with her light, power, knowledge, consciousness, Ananda, acting upon the Adhara and, when it is opened to her, pouring into it with these divine forces that makes the Sadhana possible. But so long as the lower nature is active the personal effort of the Sadhaka remains necessary."* [21]

**Question:** Sri Aurobindo has stated in many places that in his Yoga of Transformation it is only the Mother's Power, i.e. the Supramental Power, that can transform the mind, vital and body of the sadhak. But the extract quoted above *"it is the Divine who is the Sadhaka and the Sadhana"*, is difficult to understand. What is the true meaning of this statement?

**Answer:** You can discover the true meaning when you read the whole chapter. It has been clearly stated that in this yoga, *"it is the Divine who is the Sadhaka and the Sadhana"*. Sri Aurobindo said this because it is the Divine Shakti who does the yoga *"with her light, power, knowledge, consciousness, Ananda, acting upon the Adhara and, when it is opened to her, pouring into it with these divine forces . . . ."* It is these Divine Forces that make the sadhana possible and it is the Divine Power that is doing the work of sadhana. This is why Sri Aurobindo said that in this yoga the Divine is the sadhaka and the sadhana.

**Question:** In this yoga, it is the mind, vital and body that will be transformed. Therefore if you surrender the actions of the mind, vital and body, the Supramental Force will do the work of transformation. The mind develops by studying and a developed mind becomes ready for transformation. Is it correct, then, to think that sadhaks should study in order to develop their minds?

**Answer:** If your idea were correct, Sri Aurobindo, who founded the Yoga of Transformation, would have opened many schools for various kinds of studies when the Ashram first came into being. Although Sri Aurobindo came to Pondicherry in 1910, the Ashram was only established by the Mother in 1926 after she had come for the second time. The Mother opened the Ashram school in 1943 in order to give education to small children, but up till now, no school has been started for the sadhaks themselves.

If, as your idea suggests, study were necessary for the development of the mind, then similarly music, dance, art, architecture, painting, sculpture, etc., would be required for the development of the vital. If the sadhak had to learn all these things, it would take him thousands of lives to reach his goal. It does actually happen like this in the natural course of evolution, but in yoga we do not sprinkle water on each separate leaf of the tree; we pour water at the root of the tree to make it flourish. Similarly, when we surrender the mind, vital and body, the Supramental Power will transform them into instruments of the Divine Truth. Once a person is transformed, he will be united with the Divine Consciousness and no deficiency or imperfection will remain within him. This is why Sri Krishna has said in the Gita: *"This is the king-knowledge, the king-secret (the wisdom of all wisdoms, the secret of all secrets) . . . ."* [22] Nothing remains to be known if one has this Supreme Knowledge; therefore study is not essential for transformation. If we simply surrender and do nama-japa, the Supramental Force will start to work. For this reason, in this yoga we have to aspire, surrender and do nama-japa.

**Question:** It is said that we should surrender our work, and study is also work. So if we surrender our study, then won't the Supramental Force do the work of transformation?

**Answer:** You are speaking of your study as work to be surrendered to the Divine, but why not surrender the work that has already been given to you?* If you prefer to study and then neglect or abandon the work that you have been given, it means that you do not have the right attitude in your sadhana, because you are not maintaining an attitude of equality towards these two kinds of work. You have a personal liking and preference for study. This personal interest implies attachment and desire, but clearly desire and the Divine cannot coexist. If you have more interest in studying than in doing your allotted work, then neglect, slackness, dislike of the work and lack of interest will surely enter into the work as obstacles. A lack of interest in the divine work means that there will also be a lack of interest and intensity in nama-japa, aspiration and surrender for the realisation of the Divine. One cannot have equal interest in two things at once. The Mother's work is done through her organisations. If the organisation suffers, it means that the Mother's work is being neglected. Therefore, it is certainly contrary to sadhana to abandon or neglect the work that has been given by the organisation in order to study instead.

---

* This refers to sadhaks who live in the Ashram or in a centre and have been allotted work there.

If you do not neglect your allotted work in any way and if you do not have the least attachment to studying and do not give much importance to it, but study only as a means to achieve your goal in sadhana and surrender it to the Mother, then it is all right.

# The Methods of Nama-Japa

It has already been said that one can always repeat the Mother's name, *Ma*, with the help of the lips right from the beginning of the sadhana of Sri Aurobindo's Yoga of Transformation. In this way it becomes very easy for the sadhak to aspire and to surrender his whole being at the feet of the Mother. The sadhak can then recognise the different kinds of obstacles and hindrances that arise due to the attacks of the hostile forces and due to his own inner resistances, and he can see the disguised forms these obstacles frequently take. He will be able to surrender all these difficulties at the feet of the Mother. Therefore the sadhak should remain alert and conscious, constantly repeating the Mother's name with firm determination. He should not stop doing nama-japa for a single moment.

One should do nama-japa until one falls asleep at night and immediately resume it upon awaking in the morning. One should do nama-japa at all times – while washing one's face, cleaning one's teeth, drinking water, going to the bathroom, taking one's bath, washing one's clothes, eating, talking with others or doing any other activity. To be able to do this, one has to remain constantly conscious and careful and keep a firm determination. One has to remain alert while washing one's mouth, for at that time nama-japa cannot be done with the lips, so one must do it silently in the mind. Likewise, one has to be conscious while drinking water or taking food. At those times one cannot repeat the Mother's name with the help of the lips, but nama-japa will still go on in the mind. If one has to say something, one should say only what is necessary, resuming nama-japa the moment one stops talking.

It is only through nama-japa that sadhaks of all levels can be conscious right from the beginning of their sadhana. A sadhak with strong aspiration and nama-japa constantly upon his lips can save himself from the clutches of that most powerful and invincible of enemies – mechanical thoughts.

Nama-japa should be done constantly. Japa is essential in all types of yoga and has been given a very high place in all forms of sadhana, but in the Integral Yoga of Sri Aurobindo no other processes of sadhana can help except the nama-japa of *Ma,* aspiration and surrender. This is because in this yoga the Mother is both the sadhak and the sadhana, and the transformation of the sadhak's mind, vital and body into Light and Truth is impossible without her Power. The proof of this is that until now there has been no transformation of any sadhak's mind, life and body into Divine Truth and Light by means of any form of yoga or sadhana, nor has any sadhak become completely free from disease, old age and death. Moreover, the ignorance, falsehood and wrongdoings that exist in the world are still gradually increasing. But once the mind, vital and body of the sadhaks have been transformed, falsehood, injustice and wrongdoings will disappear from the world. This death-bound world will then become a Divine Heaven.

# The Effect of *Ma*-Nama-Japa

Sri Aurobindo has said: *"As a rule the only mantra used in this Sadhana is that of the Mother or of my name and the Mother's."*

The Mother has said: *"only japa has a direct action on the body."* She has also said that by means of japa alone she accomplished ten years of sadhana in a few months.

Mantra-japa is the key to sadhana and brings realisation. It also brings the realisation of the Ishta Devata, one's chosen deity. The sadhak can realise the living form of the deity whom he worships through the repetition of a particular name. This is why we say that the Ishta and the name are inseparable; one can certainly realise the Ishta Devata by doing nama-japa.

Even in the ordinary world we find that name and form are inseparable; if you call someone by his name, that person is bound to respond, even if you do not know him. Similarly, in certain mantra-rituals the deity whose name is repeated will appear.

In this yoga, the transformation is being done by the Supramental Power. The Supramental Power and the Mother are one and the same Truth. The presence of the Mother is absolutely necessary from the very beginning of this sadhana.

When the sadhak does *Ma*-nama-japa, the Mother's Power will descend into him and start the work of transformation. Indeed, the action of transformation *is* the presence of the Mother. When the work of transformation starts, the psychic being will awaken more and more, surrender will increase and aspiration will become intense. For these reasons, the japa of the Mother's name is extremely necessary. The arduous path of transformation becomes easy by the japa of *Ma*.

Here is a further explanation of why this is so. It has been stated in the scriptures that the Sanskrit letter म (M) is the bija (seed-syllable) for chandra, the moon. Chandra contains amrita, divine nectar, and is cooling and peaceful; it is the embodiment of bliss. When the sadhak repeats this seed-syllable, peace, bliss and devotion become established in his mind, vital and body. Then the hostile forces, which create obstacles in his life and are the cause of depression, greed, attachment, lust and anger, cannot easily become active. Then he obtains encouragement and happiness and takes interest in his sadhana. The obstacles become less and, as his mind, vital and body become purified, the Divine Power descends into them and starts the work of transformation.

By adding the Sanskrit letter आ (A) to the letter म (M), one gets the word मा (*Ma*). आ (A) is the seed-syllable for agni, the purifying spiritual fire. Because the letter आ (A) in the word मा (*Ma*) is the seed-syllable for the purifying spiritual fire, the sadhak's three types of karma, which are the results of his unfavourable past actions – sanchita (the results of actions from previous lives), kriyamana (the results of actions from this life) and prarabdha (the present destiny) – will be burnt away by the japa of *Ma*. When the results of all the wrong actions committed by the sadhak in life after life from the beginning of the world, are destroyed and the psychic being awakens, then the veil of ignorance, attachment and illusion is lifted from his mind, vital and body. Then, through the influence of the psychic being, his intellect becomes clear and pure, enabling him to see through the disguised forms that the adverse forces take when they try to attract him and lure him away from the path of sadhana.

Along with the constant repetition of *Ma*, one should keep a regular and fixed time for meditation. If at the time of meditation one's consciousness enters deep within the heart and the Divine Shakti starts to work in the body, then nama-japa may temporarily be discontinued if the habit of repeating the name in the place where one is concentrating or the place where the Divine Shakti is working has not yet been established. Once the habit has become established, japa should be done at all times, for if the name, *Ma*, is repeated at the place where the Divine Shakti is acting, then the Shakti can work intensely and no thoughts will be able to come.

# Meditation

The Mother and Sri Aurobindo have written about meditation in the Integral Yoga in various places in their works. They explain that it may be practised above the head, between the eyebrows or in the heart centre; but they have placed more emphasis on meditation above the head and in the heart.

When one meditates above the head, the consciousness opens upwards and ascends. Then the Powers of the Mother – Peace, Force, Light, Knowledge and Bliss – descend into the mind, life and body of the sadhak and the Divine Shakti does the work of transformation.

When one meditates in the depths of the heart, the psychic being awakens and aspires for the descent of the Divine Shakti and the surrender of the mind, life and body – that is to say, the entire being – at the feet of the Mother. The psychic being guides the sadhak to take the straight path towards the goal. This is the reason meditation in the heart is so essential.

In the book *Questions and Answers*, the Mother has made this statement about meditation:

*"Concentrate in the heart. Enter into it; go within and deep and far, as far as you can. Gather all the strings of your consciousness that are spread abroad, roll them up and take a plunge and sink down.*

*A fire is burning there, in the deep quietude of the heart. It is the divinity in you – your true being. Hear its voice, follow its dictates.*

*There are other centres of concentration, for example, one above the crown and another between the eye-brows. Each has its own efficacy and will give you a particular result. But the central being lies in the heart and from the heart proceed all central movements – all dynamism and urge for transformation and power of realisation."* [23]

If you cannot meditate according to the above method, then at the beginning you can gaze at a photograph of the Mother or a combined photograph of the Mother and Sri Aurobindo. After some time, try to see the image with your eyes closed. If you can see it clearly after closing your eyes, then visualise this picture inside your heart, and imagine yourself sitting before it. Try to concentrate upon it one-pointedly. Be determined to go deeper into the heart. If you cannot go deeper, then remain at the point you have reached. When thoughts come, do not allow them to enter, but try to keep them out. Do this for five minutes. If you can concentrate in this way easily, then try to meditate for a longer time. If thoughts come while you are meditating upon the image of the Mother, repeat her name, *Ma*, rapidly upon your lips. If you do this no thoughts will come and if you practise sincerely, one-pointedness will develop automatically. Then the image of the Mother's photograph will not remain, but the Mother's Power, Peace, Bliss and Knowledge will descend from above the head and your consciousness will start to enter into the depths of the heart. Go as deep as possible. Wherever the consciousness stops, stay there; remain there as long as you can. At that time one becomes immersed in Peace and Bliss. When the consciousness comes out of the heart, then to whatever part of the body or point or place it may go and in whatever way it may move or work, do not offer the slightest resistance, but give it your full continued support with determined willingness. Do not offer any resistance to its movements, for this is the work of transformation by the Divine Shakti.

In this yoga, the descent of the Divine Shakti and the work of transformation cannot be achieved by meditation alone. It has already been stated that aspiration and surrender are the keys to and foundation of this yoga. By repeating the Mother's name, *Ma*, aspiration and surrender become easy and the mind, vital and body slowly become purified. Then the psychic being awakens, and when it awakens it aspires. In response to its aspiration, the Divine Shakti descends from above and begins the work of transformation in the being of the sadhak. In the initial stages, the work of transformation is slow; thoughts from outside enter the mind and interrupt the work of transformation by the Divine Power. At such times, instead of identifying with the thoughts that come, the sadhak should mentally repeat the name, *Ma*, without moving his lips, at the place where the Divine Shakti is working. Then thoughts will not intervene and the action of the Divine Shakti will become more intense.

# The Greatness of Nama-Japa

The Mother has said: *"I have also come to realise that for this sadhana of the body, the mantra is essential . . . because only japa has a direct action on the body."* [24]

In *Mother's Agenda*, the Mother was asked the following question: *"But for us who want an integral realisation, are all these mantras and this daily japa really a help, or do they also shut us in?"*

The Mother replied: *"It gives discipline. It's an almost subconscious discipline of the character more than of thought.*

*Especially at the beginning, Sri Aurobindo used to shatter to pieces all moral ideas (you know, as in the Aphorisms, for example). He shattered all those things, he shattered them, really shattered them to pieces. So there's a whole group of youngsters here who were brought up with this idea that 'we can do whatever we want, it doesn't matter in the least!' – that they need not bother about all those concepts of ordinary morality. I've had a hard time making them understand that this morality can be abandoned only for a higher one . . . . So, one has to be careful not to give them the Power too soon.*

*It's an almost physical discipline. Moreover, I have seen that the japa has an organizing effect on the subconscient, on the inconscient, on matter, on the body's cells – it takes time, but by persistently repeating it, in the long run it has an effect. It is the same principle as doing daily exercises on the piano, for example. You keep mechanically repeating them, and in the end your hands are filled with consciousness – it fills the body with consciousness."* [25]

She also said: *"To the most stubborn goes the victory.*

*When I started my japa one year ago, I had to struggle with every possible difficulty, every contradiction, prejudice and opposition that fills the air. And even when this poor body began walking back and forth for japa, it used to knock against things, it would start breathing all wrong, coughing; it was attacked from all sides until the day I caught the Enemy and said, 'Listen carefully. You can do whatever you want, but I'm going right to the end and nothing will stop me, even if I have to repeat this mantra ten crore\* times.' The result was really miraculous, like a cloud of bats flying up into the light all at once. From that moment on, things started going better."* [26]

The Mother has given the foremost place to japa in the practice of the Yoga of Transformation. She has said that for the transformation of the body, surrender and aspiration are insufficient, that *"the purely psychological method is inadequate and that a japa is necessary, because only japa has a direct action on the body."* Moreover, she has said that through japa she had done *"ten years of work in a few months".* [27]

Again the Mother has said: *"In fact, you can immediately see the difference between those who have a mantra and those who don't. With those who have no mantra, even if they have a strong habit of meditation or*

---

\* One crore = 10 million

*concentration, something around them remains hazy and vague. Whereas the japa imparts to those who practise it a kind of precision, a kind of solidity: an armature. They become galvanised, as it were."* [28]

From this it can be clearly understood that the Mother has given the highest place to japa in the process of transforming the body. It is only through nama-japa that a sadhak can easily remain constantly conscious, that surrender and aspiration, which are so difficult, can be achieved with less effort and that one-pointedness develops automatically. And it is only through japa that the sadhak can, with little effort, become free from mechanical thoughts, which are so difficult to overcome. By the power of the name, the sadhak will be protected from all kinds of obstacles, from danger, suffering, pain and distress and from the attacks of the adverse forces. Then he will be able to proceed on the path to the goal with enthusiasm, interest and happiness. Therefore it is absolutely necessary that we do nama-japa ceaselessly.

# Introduction to Part Two

Part Two of the book *Nama-Japa in the Yoga of Transformation* by Sri Ramkrishna Das is a selection compiled from a sadhak's diary maintained during the last 10 years of Babaji's life. In most cases, Babaji's answers to questions were written down from memory shortly afterwards.

The first article titled *The Aim of Life*, is based on several Satsangs (spiritual discourses) given by Babaji during the last week of December 1990. It is followed by questions and answers concerning the practice of Sri Aurobindo's yoga. Furthermore, some anecdotes and experiences with Babaji that highlight his personality and his achievements in this yoga are also included.

It is hoped that practitioners will feel inspired to follow Babaji's advice of constantly repeating the Mother's name, *Ma*.

# Babaji Maharaj Ramkrishna Das

For many of us, Babaji was the embodiment of love and humility. His room was very simple; he himself always wore only a white sleeveless undershirt and half of a white dhoti (one dhoti cut into 2 pieces). He used to sit on a small, low stool, and if anybody approached him with a question or for some help, Babaji would turn towards that person with so much love and compassion that one had the feeling as if nobody else existed in this world but Babaji and oneself. It was the most amazing experience. On the other hand one's questions and doubts would often simply dissolve just by entering his room without any outward conversation having taken place. A single glance full of compassion and love would be enough.

In 1961, the Mother gave an answer to the following question:

*"I would like to know by what signs such a person {who is in touch with the Supermind} can be recognized?"*

Mother replied: … *"but I can tell you right away that there are two signs – two certain, infallible signs. I know them through personal experience, for they are two things that can ONLY come with the supramental consciousness; without it, one cannot possess them – no yogic effort, no discipline, no tapasya can give them to you, while they come almost automatically with the supramental consciousness.*
*The first sign is perfect equality as Sri Aurobindo has described it … exactly as he described it with such wonderful precision! But this equality (which is not*

*'equanimity') is a particular STATE where one relates to all things, outer and inner, and to each individual thing, in the same way. That is truly perfect equality: vibrations from things, from people, from contacts have no power to alter that state...*

*The second sign is a sense of ABSOLUTENESS in knowledge.... This state CANNOT be obtained through any region of the mind, even the most illumined and exalted. It's... not a 'certainty', it's (Mother lowers both hands like an irresistible block descending), a kind of absoluteness, without even any possibility of hesitation (there's no question of doubt), or anything like that."*[29]

To those who were in close contact with Babaji and under his guidance, the Mother's answer doubtlessly applied to him.

Here is a telling entry from the sadhak's diary:

"Babaji almost always wore a hat on his head, and I sometimes wondered why he would do so even if the outside temperature was 35 degrees Celsius or more.

One afternoon, I entered Babaji's room with a very pressing question regarding some personal problem. I found Babaji alone in his room, sitting as usual on his little wooden stool. That afternoon, perhaps because he was alone, he was not wearing his hat. I bowed down to him and sat on the floor next to him. Babaji bent down to me and asked me with his infinite compassion what the matter was. At this moment the top of his head was almost at my eye level. Babaji's head was mostly bald, with a few strands of silvery hair here and there; he was over 80 years old. I told him my problem. Babaji listened intently, and the whole world receded into the background.

After I had spoken, there was a moment of silence before Babaji answered. As he began to speak, I suddenly saw that the centre of the top of his head, what here in India is known as the thousand-petalled lotus at the crown of the head opened and began to pulsate. It was as if there was no bone at all just some pulsating hole covered with skin. At this moment, I knew without a shadow of a doubt that whatever Babaji was saying was coming directly from the Mother. That he had made contact and was now functioning as a channel between me and the Mother.

The experience was completely overwhelming for me, and thereafter I never had any doubt that whatever Babaji advised came directly from the Mother, and I always tried to follow his advice implicitly."

One can draw an analogy to those early TV sets. If they did not have an antenna, all one would receive was a bunch of snow on a glimmering screen without any image. Babaji was our antenna and tirelessly he stooped down to our level to help us advance.

# The Aim of Life and Sri Aurobindo's Yoga

What is the aim of life? Were we to ask this question to a number of individuals, each one would probably come up with a different answer. For example, one person may tell us that his or her aim in life is to become a good doctor, while another one may want to become a successful businessman. A third person's aim in life may be to earn lots of money, become a good mother or father, be a sportsman, a famous artist or musician, etc. In the end, we would find that each person has his or her own particular aim in life. But what is it that lies hidden behind all these various aims?

What is it that we are all individually seeking? Would it not be true to say that all these individual life-aims are strung together by one common, underlying wish, the wish for happiness? Are we not pursuing whatever we have chosen to do in life in the hope that this will make us happy? Indeed, could we possibly find even a single human being on earth who does not want happiness?

We would then have to conclude that everyone in the world, from the youngest to the oldest, from the most illiterate and ignorant to the most developed and educated is seeking to be happy, and we can therefore say that this without exception, is the only aim of life common to everyone. However, in the entire history of humanity, have we ever succeeded in achieving this single universal aim? The answer of course is 'no, we have not'.

Over and above our own individual struggles and hardships which constantly mar or even destroy our happiness, we are confronted with three major universal obstacles that stand across our path. These three obstacles are old age, disease, and death. From his earliest beginnings until the present day man has ceaselessly struggled to prolong his youth, to conquer all diseases, and to ward off death, and he shall continue to do so in the future.

If in our day to day life we attempt to achieve a certain end but encounter repeated failure, we eventually give up trying and divert our attention towards some other goal. For example, after failing a college entrance examination several times, we eventually resign ourselves to this fact, give up the endeavour and turn our attention to something else. But contrary to this humanity as a whole in its quest for everlasting happiness, has never given up trying and will forever continue trying to overcome these three obstacles of disease, old age, and death. How can this be explained?

We may observe that our thoughts never dwell too long on the evident fact that in the course of time we will age, fall ill, and inevitably die. Strangely enough, we never ask ourselves with any determined persistence why it should be that way. Subconsciously, we refuse to acknowledge these facts and thus they appear to us like a dream, like something that in its essence cannot be true. How can this be explained?

It is because something deep within us knows that everlasting happiness is the birthright of every human being. Concealed deep within us, not known to our outer consciousness dwells this truth which is not, has never been, and will never be afflicted by suffering, old age, disease and death and which is the hidden cause of humanity's ceaseless quest and ever-continuing attempt to achieve everlasting happiness.

The central aim of western science, for example, is to understand life, conquer the elements, and gain control over life and death. But have they succeeded in this? Have we, in all our individual efforts to obtain lasting happiness in our lives succeeded? I may have become the doctor or businessman I wanted to be, and I may be happy with this achievement, but does this happiness have any lasting stability? Is it not constantly shaken by events that are beyond my control? One of my family members may fall seriously ill. I may have an accident. Someone may speak badly about me. A person close to me may die. My child's behaviour may go beyond my control. Under such circumstances, can I sustain that perfect happiness which I had hoped for? Am I not constantly plagued by the fear of losing it?

If we turn our attention to the East, we discover another ancient method used in the quest for everlasting happiness. The different yoga paths practised for centuries in different parts of Asia had as their sole aim the inner realisation of God in order to escape the turmoil and ups and downs of ordinary life and gain a permanent state of peace and happiness. Aspirants believed that this was not possible to obtain within life, that there was no way to change this world or human nature which would forever be subject to pain and suffering. They therefore removed themselves from worldly life, cut all attachments to family and friends, and went to some remote place where they practised severe and arduous disciplines concentrating exclusively on their goal to realise the Divine. This was only possible by detaching themselves not only from the world but also from the desires, demands, and workings of their mind, vital, and body. By means of an intense inward and upward concentration, the seekers of the traditional yoga paths separated their consciousness from mind, vital, and body and went into higher planes, leaving mind, life, and body behind. Through this process they became aware of their soul, which is an eternal part of the Supreme.

But only a few people were able to undergo such strict disciplines and succeed. Those who succeeded gained an inner state of permanent happiness. This happiness, however, was not integral. It was the happiness of the inner being, separate from the person's mind, life, and body which remained almost as ignorant and untransformed as before. As soon as the aspirant participated in worldly life, as occasions arose, they continued to be subject to frustration, unhappiness, anger etc. as well as old age, disease, and death. Furthermore, the happiness achieved through the various methods of yoga was purely individual and had no bearing on the world, which remained as before in a state of strife and turmoil. The realised souls could not pass on their achievements to humanity as a whole. They could only lead a few others whom they had accepted as their disciples along the same arduous path to inner salvation. The traditional yoga paths could not be practised by everyone and could not give the answer to mankind's quest for overcoming old age, disease, and death.

Though we recognise that the sole aim of life is to achieve everlasting happiness for all of mankind, we are ignorant of the path that will lead us there, and we try out various methods according to our nature, understanding, likes and dislikes. But we do not know the right method and, therefore, despite all our endeavours, we experience much suffering. The cause of this suffering lies in the very nature of our ignorant mind, life, and body, and only if their nature is transformed into their true Divine Nature can we establish in us lasting peace and happiness.

If a never-ending state of well-being is the true aim of life for everyone, the method to obtain it must be one that can be practised by all, under any circumstances, regardless of age, sex, religion, culture, education, language, etc. It must be a method not apart from human life in some remote forest, undergoing severe austerities, but a method that is part and parcel of life, practicable for all, which will bring permanent happiness into life on earth, and which will as its crowning goal, conquer old age, disease, and death, those three obstacles that seem to permanently bar our way.

Sri Aurobindo says that *"All life is Yoga"*[30] and he has given us the method by which to arrive at our quest for happiness. His method is not an individual one divorced from life, cut off from mind, life, and body, but a collective method that works within life and includes every facet of our human existence. According to Sri Aurobindo, the goal of this worldly creation is the establishment of a divine life on earth - not an individual inner salvation, but a heaven on earth - through the divinization of life, mind and body.

In one of his *Letters on Yoga*, Sri Aurobindo writes: *"The old Yoga demanded a complete renunciation extending to the giving up of the worldly life itself. This yoga aims instead at a new and transformed life ... Its aim is to refound life in the truth of the spirit and for that purpose to transfer the roots of all we are and do from the mind, life and body to a greater consciousness above the mind."*[31]

Life, mind and body have therefore to be transformed and raised out of their ignorance and darkness into the divine light and truth.

Sri Aurobindo says: *"It must be remembered that for the divine life on earth, earth and Matter have not to be and cannot be rejected but have only to be sublimated and to reveal in themselves the possibilities of the spirit, serve the spirit's highest uses and be transformed into instruments of a greater living."* [32]
But how do we arrive at this possibility of transformation of mind, life and body?

Sri Aurobindo answers: *"It is indeed as a result of our evolution that we arrive at the possibility of this transformation. As Nature has evolved beyond Matter and manifested Life, beyond Life and manifested Mind, so she must evolve beyond Mind and manifest a consciousness and power of our existence free from the imperfection and limitation of our mental existence, a supramental or truth-consciousness, and able to develop the power and perfection of the spirit. ... Into that truth we shall be freed and it will transform mind and life and body."*[33]

Sri Aurobindo and the Mother took birth in a human body to usher in this next step in our evolution. They brought down and established here upon earth the Supramental Force which will transform mind, life, and body and eventually conquer old age, disease, and death. It is this Supramental Truth-Consciousness that is our birthright and which we have been ignorantly searching for since time immemorial.

If we understand and accept this aim of life, we must then look for the path that will lead us towards it.

In his book *The Mother* Sri Aurobindo writes: *"There are two powers that alone can effect in their conjunction the great and difficult thing which is the aim of our endeavour, a fixed and unfailing aspiration that calls from below and a supreme Grace from above that answers."*[34]

This means there has to be on our part, firstly, an acceptance of the true aim of life, and a call for this truth to come and manifest in our lives. Only if we aspire for the divine Grace, Truth, Light and Knowledge, will an opening be created within ourselves that makes it possible for the divine Grace to act. Left to our own endeavour we cannot achieve the difficult transformation of our mind, life, and body. Only the direct action of the divine Grace can bring about this change in our lives.

*"But"*, Sri Aurobindo writes, *"the supreme Grace will act only in the conditions of the Light and the Truth; ..."*[35]

This means that the divine Grace cannot act in conditions where there is no opening through which it can enter and do its work. What, then, are the conditions of the Light and Truth?

Sri Aurobindo says: *"These are the conditions of the Light and Truth, the sole conditions under which the very highest Force will descend; and it is only the very highest supramental Force descending from above and opening from below that can victoriously handle the physical Nature and annihilate its difficulties ... There must be a total and sincere surrender; there must be an exclusive self-opening to the divine Power; there must be a constant and integral choice of the Truth that is descending, a constant and integral rejection of the falsehood of the mental, vital and physical Powers and Appearances that still rule the earth-Nature."*[36]

Having accepted the transformation of mind, vital and body as the ultimate aim of life, we may yet feel that the conditions necessary for the Light and Truth to transform us are impossible to fulfil. How can we surrender sincerely and totally? How can we open ourselves exclusively to the divine Power? How can we constantly and integrally choose the Truth that is descending and integrally reject all falsehood of the mental, vital and physical Powers and Appearances? Do we not have to conclude that these conditions are impossible for us to fulfil, that this yoga and this aim of life are not possible for all to achieve?

This is not so. Sri Aurobindo's writings are aimed at aspirants of all different levels and stages of development. While in one place he gives guidance to beginners, in another place his writings are meant for intermediaries or for persons who have already advanced on the path of this yoga. The conditions Sri Aurobindo is describing in the above quote are meant for advanced aspirants who have already purified their mind, vital and body and are therefore ready to receive this highest Supramental Force into their being, so that it may do its work of transformation.

We, who are at the beginning stage of this yoga, should not feel perturbed by these conditions. All that is asked of us in the beginning is the sincere acceptance of the idea of Truth. Then, as we gradually proceed on the path, we will, after a shorter or longer time, automatically be able to fulfil the required conditions.

Since this yoga is for all, the initial acceptance of this ideal and aim of life is not tied to any conditions. Anybody can accept it, whatever his or her position in life. Once we accept the aim, we slowly start aspiring for it. This aspiration will call down into our being a ray of light which will work in us and help us to clearly understand the purpose of all life. Slowly our aspiration will grow in intensity, and we will be able to reject unhelpful habits, desires, and thoughts, and surrender them to the Mother.* The practice of this growing aspiration, rejection and surrender is the personal effort which the aspirant is asked to make so that the divine Grace may be able to act. As our mind turns more and more towards the Divine, asking for his help, we can rely on one sure and simple method that will bring us gradually and safely to the goal.

It is the constant remembrance of the Mother and the constant calling of her name, 'Ma', (which is as powerful as her physical presence) in all our day to day activities, remembering that she is with us, helping us at every moment. When we take a bath, brush our teeth, sweep the floor, work, play, eat, or before going to sleep, if we constantly repeat the Mother's name, 'Ma', she will be with us at all times, protecting us always and guiding us safely towards our goal according to our own capacity, intensity of aspiration and need. Never mind how manifold our imperfections are, or how deep our ignorance is, if we constantly call her, offering to her all our difficulties and all our incapacities, she will help us to proceed and free us from the defects of our ignorant lower nature.

This yoga is not to suppress life or to suppress our

---

* The One whom we adore as the Mother is the divine Conscious Force that dominates all existence..." Sri Aurobindo, *The Mother with Letters on the Mother*, p.14, 2012

habits and desires, but to offer them to the Mother so that she may purify and transform our mind, vital and body. The more we remember her and rely on her, the swifter and safer this period of purification will be.

If we aspire for the Truth wholeheartedly, the Divine accepts us without any conditions.
Gradually, as our aspiration grows, our faith in and dependence on the Mother will also grow, and it is She who will pave the way and slowly remove the obstacles in our nature and purify our being to such an extent that we will eventually be able to obey the conditions of the Light and Truth which make the descent of the highest Supramental Force into our mind, life and body possible, where it will do the work of transformation. This transformation is complete when the mind, vital, and body have each realised the Divine and thus, a divine life on earth will have been made possible.

The swiftness with which we can advance on the path depends on our personal effort of aspiration, rejection, and surrender, on our offering of ourselves as we are to the Mother, on our reliance on her, and on our faith in her constant help.

Sri Aurobindo says: *"The more complete your faith, sincerity and surrender, the more will grace and protection be with you. And when the grace and protection of the Divine Mother are with you, what is there that can touch you or whom need you fear? A little of it even will carry you through all difficulties, obstacles and dangers; surrounded by its full presence you can go securely on your way because it is hers, careless of all menace, unaffected by any hostility however powerful, whether from this world or from worlds invisible. Its touch can turn difficulties into opportunities, failure into success and weakness into unfaltering strength. For the grace of the Divine Mother is the sanction of the Supreme and now or tomorrow its effect is sure, a thing decreed, inevitable and irresistible."*[37]

Babaji

# How do we begin?

**Babaji:** There is only one God. Before the creation there was only He. (**Note:** God is neither male nor female, gender-specific pronouns are used in the conventional way to make understanding easier.) Then God decided to manifest himself through his creation and divided himself into two parts: the Shakti, the active, creative force, and Brahman, the static part above the creation.

Creation began:
Out of darkness matter evolved, out of matter plant life evolved, out of that the animal kingdom and beyond, the human creation evolved. The vital principle is fully evolved in the animal kingdom, while the full development of the mind belongs to the human creation. Mind, however, has the capacity to destroy the creation, and it is always at such crucial times that the Divine (the Avatar) descends to earth in a human body to save the world. However, the influence of the past divine descents was not strong enough to change human nature, and only a few people profited directly from these special divine incarnations.

Mind is now fully evolved in man and cannot evolve further. A fourth principle is already active to bring man's soul, which is far above the mind, to the forefront so that it may transform mind, life, and body into their true divine nature. Sri Aurobindo and the Mother came to earth to establish here this fourth principle, the Supramental Force, which is now acting on the whole world, not only on a section of humanity. Even without practising yoga this force will eventually, in the course of evolution, over perhaps millions of years, change and transform humanity.

God is all-powerful. He could change the whole world immediately, but He bows down to the evolutionary laws of nature. He descends into a human body and subjects himself to those laws in order to change them, at the same time giving man the possibility to approach and serve Him.

In this lifetime, we are given a special opportunity as there is a very special pressure for change. Now we can make much progress in a short time, which may otherwise take thousands of years.

All our difficulties are within ourselves. They are our ego, our selfishness, our pride, etc. If we can recognise these things within us and reject these movements without expressing them in action, we will have peace even long before these movements are transformed.

**Babaji:** The animal is ruled by its vital; human beings are also mostly under the control of their vital. The more developed and educated a person is, the more will his mind attempt to control his vital using prevailing moral and religious rules as guidelines. But still, often the vital gets its way over the mind.

Human beings are the most evolved on the

evolutionary scale, with mind being the last step in the evolution. The mind of a scientist is highly evolved; it has reached the end of its human evolution. Mind cannot go any further than this. A new principle is necessary for human beings to evolve further and go beyond the principle of mind.

This new principle is the soul-power. The Supramental Force is necessary to bring the soul to the fore so that it may govern mind, life, and body, and transform and evolve human beings into Supramental Beings. This cannot be done by the powers of the mind. Therefore, Sri Aurobindo and the Mother came to earth to establish here the Supramental Power. This power is now actively working, and with our efforts of aspiration, rejection and surrender, it will transform us.

**Babaji:** At present, the adverse forces are ruling the world, they are dominating it. But these adverse forces are not able to work in a void, they use human beings as their instruments.

The Supramental Force has now touched every human being. Because of this, mankind has become acutely conscious of its suffering and pain, and while previously man accepted them as part of life and did not think too much about them, he is now trying to find ways to free himself from this suffering and pain. But since he does not know how to do so, we see all kinds of chaos and wars in the world.
Increasingly though, people are becoming conscious

and are no longer living in total ignorance. As more and more people become conscious, the power of the adverse forces will decline because they will no longer be able to use these human beings as their instruments.

The divine power is much stronger than the power of the adversaries. Therefore, it will not need the collaboration of the entire earth-population to destroy the adverse forces. A few people are enough. Nevertheless, change will happen much faster if many people accept this yoga. Within 50 years from now (1988), we will see big changes in the world. Already we have seen how the Divine Forces averted the Third World War during the Cuba crisis.

**Question**: Does one need to develop one's mind to the fullest first in order to pass beyond?

**Babaji:** To be able to grow into superhuman levels, one does not need to have a fully developed mind. Once this force starts working, the mind will become even more developed than that of a scientist. The aim of life has to be clear in one's mind, and there has to be a strong desire within us to reach it.

It is also important to understand the difference between Sri Aurobindo's and the Mother's yoga and the traditional paths. It is not so easy to understand, and the mind may know at one time and then become unclear again.

**Question:** What is the universal self?

**Babaji:** The personal self is derived from the universal self. There is a universal mind, a universal vital, and a universal body. Our personal mind, vital and body are directly connected to the universal. If we conquer one aspect of our lower vital nature, we have also gained a victory in the universal vital. Thus, slowly, the universal mind, vital and body will be transformed; therefore it is good if many people practise this sadhana. It becomes easier, and the transformation proceeds faster. If only a few people practise the sadhana, the transformation will still be done, but it will take a longer time.

Once the universal mind, vital, and body are transformed, then Supramental Beings can appear and we will have heaven on earth for everyone. Even though for human beings this universal mind, vital and body will still exist, its essence will be totally different. There will no longer be anger, jealousy, ill-will, etc. in the universal nature. Instead, there will be harmony, compassion, understanding, and goodwill. And since the personal self is connected to the universal self, there will be only peace and happiness on earth. Even the wild animals will change. They will kill only for their own survival. Harmony will prevail between man and nature, and a cobra, for example, will not bite you. Plants will reveal their special purpose and properties.

In the same way that an animal cannot imagine what it will be like to be a human being, we cannot imagine what it will be like when Supramental Beings are on earth.

In this sadhana, we all help each other. The more advanced sadhaks also profit from the beginners. As the beginners take up the fight against the lower universal nature, the burden is lightened for the more advanced sadhaks so that they can then pursue more advanced stages of sadhana.

**Question**: When the first Supramental Beings will be on earth, will humans, animals and plant-life remain?

**Babaji**: Yes.

**Question**: Forever?

**Babaji**: Yes, the evolution will always continue, but it will be very different. There won't be any more wars, all fighting will stop and all the people will live happily. Satya Yuga, the age of Truth, will continue forever. Procreation and death will remain for human beings and some persons might get diseases which will be cured by natural ways and medicines.

**Question**: Will human beings recognize Supramental Beings?

**Babaji**: Yes, those beings will be very different from humans. Their bodies will be very different.

They will not procreate in the human way. Human beings and Supramental Beings will live peacefully side by side. At that time all suffering and pain will stop for humanity who will then grow and evolve from light to more light.

**Question**: What exactly is the Psychic Being?

**Babaji**: The Psychic Being is a part of God, while mind, life and body are instruments of the ignorance. The Psychic Being is in the background, and lets the other parts live their lives.

When the Psychic Being awakens, at that time the person turns towards God. As the Psychic grows, it exerts pressure on mind, life and body. In the measure that these parts surrender the Psychic Being takes over the lead and we become conscious of it. It then takes over the sadhana. When all the parts of our being are psychicised, a higher force descends and spiritualises mind, vital and body. After that, the Supramental Force will do its work of transformation.

**Question**: What is the difference between the Psychic Being and the soul?

**Babaji**: Sri Aurobindo referred to the soul as the Atman, the highest reality above the head which is constant and not involved in the evolution.

The Psychic Being is behind our heart and is involved in the evolution. It starts out as a little flame developing more and more from life to life until finally it is fully organized, and having taken on a shape it begins to exert pressure on the mind, vital and body.

In matter, plant, and animal life the Psychic is not present as a being, it is present as a spirit or spark. Only in human life does it slowly evolve into a fully organized being.

**Question**: What exactly does it mean to realize God in the vital?

**Babaji**: Now the vital is full of desires. At that time it will not have any more desires, it will want what God wants.

**Question**: And to realize God in the physical?

**Babaji**: This means the transformation of the body which cannot be done in a short time. It means that the body will want what God wants. Now the mind tells the body what to do. When God is realised in the physical, then the body will move on its own without the intervention of the mind.

But we need not worry! Now we experience time as a pressure, because we experience sorrow and suffering. But when we realize God and have surrendered everything to Him, then difficulties will still come, but we will remain happy because we know that God will take care of us. We will always be happy, and therefore time is no longer a pressure. The sense of time changes and we no longer care whether the transformation takes 50,000 years or 100,000 years.

In this world there is not one person who is truly happy. Happiness can only come in the spiritual life.

**Question**: What exactly is aspiration, rejection and surrender?

**Babaji:** Surrender is the attitude that all we are and all we have belongs to the Divine, since the Divine is in everything and has created it. Our body belongs to the Divine, all we do belongs to the Divine and should be surrendered to Him. The will to constantly keep and realize this attitude is aspiration. Rejection means to reject all movements (such as anger, jealousy, ill-will towards others etc.) which contradict this attitude and work against it.

It is very difficult to always remember and practise these three things. We can do it only if we constantly repeat the Mother's name, 'Ma'. Then it becomes easy. The mind is not able to understand these things because they are not within the domain or function and purpose of the mind. Only the heart can feel them.

**Question**: Is it possible to realize God in this lifetime?

**Babaji:** It is possible to realize God in one life. It all depends on the person, on the circumstances, one's past samskaras (old habitual tendencies) and one's past lives. It can be done in one month, one year, one life or many lives, depending on how sincerely one wants it and aspires for it. But even if one is not able to surrender everything in this life, once a person has turned to God, even if he leaves Him half way, God will never leave this person.

The possibility to realize God does not depend on one's purity but on one's want and need and sincerity. One has to be clear about the aim. Our aim is to realize God in mind, life and body. "Realizing God" means to have complete faith and dependence on Him, to know always and in all circumstances that the Divine will take care of us.

For example, one may have faith in one's mind and vital, but standing in front of a lion our physical may still tremble. This is because complete faith and dependence have not yet fully descended into the physical. Once this faith is also completely established in the physical, there can be no more fear and no more suffering.
If we have complete faith in and dependence on God in our mind, life and body, then all suffering

and unhappiness will stop forever. Even though realization of God may take place in one lifetime, transformation cannot take place in just one lifetime.* For those sadhaks who sincerely practise this sadhana and repeat the Mother's name always, difficulties will be nil.

Our faith and dependence in the beginning are not perfect, but by aspiration, rejection and surrender and by constantly doing japa, they will develop. The most important thing is to do japa always, to always repeat the name, everything else is bound to come.

**\*Note:** Babaji completely changed this statement a few years later. In 1997, Babaji said that nobody can imagine at what tremendous speed this Force is working, and therefore everything has now changed and complete transformation is now possible in just one lifetime. Two conditions will have to be met: one must want it and one must give oneself completely to the Mother with faith and dependence.

**Question:** I want to know whether realization can be achieved in one life, so that I can fix my aim firmly in my mind.

**Babaji:** No, this is not the right idea, it comes from the ego. Do not think in this way. All that is necessary is to surrender by thinking: "Mother, I am yours, I belong to you. Mother is always with me, she will save me", and to constantly repeat her name, 'Ma'. This is what you have to practice, it is all that is needed, everything else will come of its own. We might read books about this or that method, but it will not be useful. The only thing is to think: "Mother, I am yours, Mother will save me."

**Question**: How do we know that the effort we are making is not ego?

**Babaji**: If you think that you are the only one who can do this work, that you are doing it best, then that is the ego. You have to think, this is the Mother's work, I am doing this work for her.

There are three stages of work when one does sadhana. During the first stage, one offers one's work to the Mother, but one feels that one is the doer and one offers what one is doing. At the second stage, work is done on the divine impulse and inspiration. At that time we feel that the Divine is the doer and we are his instruments. We are aware of the Divine doing the work through us. In the first stage there is ego but there is no ego in the second stage.

In the third stage God and we are one. We do not feel any separation even though we are here upon earth. This can only come when the transformation is complete.

**Question:** Does one have to climb all the various steps that Sri Aurobindo describes in order to reach the Supermind?

**Babaji:** Before the descent of the Supermind, these steps were necessary stages. One had to go up to it as if one was climbing a staircase, meeting the various layers of consciousness and finally reaching the top. But now, Supermind has come down to earth and one can meet it directly on the "ground floor" where we are standing. It is because of this that the yoga is now possible for everyone.

**Question:** Sometimes we feel a sort of uneasiness within us, but we do not know why. At that time, should one think about it in order to find the cause of this uneasiness?

**Babaji:** No, do not think about it, do japa and surrender the feeling to the Mother. Surrendering means to think: "I am Mother's. Mother, I am yours! Mother is always with me and will always protect me!" Repeat the name very quickly, and do not think about the problem, then the adverse feeling will be removed.

If we do sadhana sincerely, which means if we are regular in our daily routine, if we sleep at the right time, get up at the right time, take a bath at the right time, eat at the right time, do our work sincerely, meditate and always do japa, everything will be all right.

When movements arise within from the lower nature such as desire, anger, ill-will, jealousy etc., do not give them any outward expression. At this time call the Mother and repeat her name very quickly so that no thoughts can come.

There will be times when we feel happy and confident and are full of faith. Then, all of a sudden, something comes up and we start to doubt and feel discouraged and all kinds of thoughts begin to disturb us. At such times do not get upset and do not despair, but hold on to your faith and tell yourself that these disturbing movements have come up for transformation.

**Question:** If one feels uneasy in one's mind or vital or body, does this mean that one is not surrendered in these parts?

**Babaji:** Yes, this is quite true, but surrender of all the parts of the being cannot be achieved in a few days. It takes time and continues all the way up to the final transformation.

One has to reject these movements that make us feel uneasy, offer them to the Mother and think that these negative feelings are not me, that I belong to the Mother and not to those forces that attack me.

At that moment, one has to call the Mother and do Nama-Japa quickly, and not pay too much attention to the difficulty.

**Question**: Sometimes this thought comes that I am not really receptive, and then I feel upset.

**Babaji:** No, no! This is a wrong thought! Any person who comes to the Divine and has offered his life, is accepted by Him, in spite of the aspirant's weaknesses or past wrongdoings. The Divine does not look at the weaknesses and wrongdoings of a person but accepts the person as he is. Imagine a burglar who stole a piece of gold and tied it securely around his waist. In a similar manner God ties us securely to Himself, regardless of our weaknesses.

**Question**: Many times we feel fear, anger, anxiety etc. but we do not understand from where these feelings are coming.

**Babaji:** Yes, this happens to everyone, because it is the nature of the mind, vital and body to feel like that.

**Question**: But at the time when one feels them, one gets identified with these feelings and begins to doubt oneself.

**Babaji:** Yes, all our reactions are habits of nature. They have not formed only in this life, but in many past lives and we have identified ourselves with them. But now even though these reactions have been formed since so many lives and for so many lives we have identified ourselves with them, the time has come, when we can free ourselves for ever from these adverse feelings and reactions in this very lifetime by doing our sadhana sincerely.

**Question:** Babaji, but what about our reactions to physical pain or illness?

**Babaji:** This worrying about one's health is a habit from all our past lives. We should just not care too much when we feel a little unwell, but go on with our daily routine. We have to think that Mother is always with us. If we do sadhana, the Force is always with us. Let the Divine take care of the body. It is His responsibility. We take medicines only as a support while offering ourselves to the Divine.

Now that we are all here, I want to say something. The most important thing for everyone is to live a spiritual life. Lasting peace without it is impossible. The time has come to spread this yoga. The more persons practise this sadhana, the easier the path will become. We have to do sadhana ourselves with firm determination and tell others about it, who will also start to aspire and spread the word as well. Gradually more and more people will begin to practice this yoga.

**Question**: When two sadhaks aspire equally, but one is in the Ashram in Pondicherry and the other one is far away, does the one in Pondy progress quicker?

**Babaji**: The Supramental Force is the Mother's force, and it is now established all over the earth, which means that Mother's presence is everywhere. Even though here in Pondicherry the atmosphere is pure because Mother and Sri Aurobindo lived here, it does not necessarily mean that one can advance here faster or further in one's sadhana than somewhere else in the world. The progress in one's sadhana does not depend on the place, but on one's intense need and one's sincerity.

It happens that sadhaks who live far away make more effort just because they are far away and they want to progress as much as sadhaks who are here. On the other hand, persons who live here are often not aware of the great privilege and the exceptional place they are living in and do not make very much effort to advance. There are sadhaks here who make no progress at all.

**Question**: If one lives here in the Ashram and offers voluntary work for the Mother, how then can ego and selfishness work?

**Babaji:** If one is not conscious, they can work very well! When thoughts come such as 'oh, I do such good work' or that one wants to become a great sadhak etc. then, together with the work, one's ego will greatly increase and become very big.

**Question:** Then, how to distinguish whether something is ego or not and how to get rid of the ego?

**Babaji:** In the beginning it is very difficult to recognise the play of one's ego because mind, vital and body are completely wrapped up in ego and selfishness. When one begins to observe one's ego and thoughts come of being a great sadhak one should immediately offer this thought to the Mother for transformation. One has to have complete faith and dependence on the Mother, then one will begin to see these ego movements.

Now we see ourselves as separate beings: I, my person, my money, my family, my relations, etc. Whenever we say 'I' we mean our mind, vital and body. We do not include in this 'I' our Psychic Being. Once we become aware of our Psychic Being then we know that we are 'That' and not mind, vital and body. Slowly the ego will get transformed and the person will become divine.

**Question:** At work, when we see that someone is making a mistake or doing things in an awkward way, should we say something to the person or will this activate our ego?

**Babaji:** First of all, we have to make sure that we have sympathy and total goodwill for the person concerned and are interested in his progress. Out of this genuine goodwill for the person, we can calmly point out his mistake. But if we encounter any resistance from the other person we should not insist on our point, we should become silent and leave it up to the Mother. Even the Divine does not interfere and remains silent if the right moment to change someone has not yet come. So who are we to think that we can change someone?

A group of people was sitting in Babaji's room. Babaji asked whether there were any questions, but nobody asked anything. After a short silence Babaji said calmly but with much force:

"Repeat the Name! Mother is always there, always helping! When difficulties come, repeat the Name! BELIEVE! Mother is always there, BELIEVE IT!"

Babaji gave the following instructions to a sadhak: "Repeat the Mother's name always, meditate two times a day for 10 minutes, 20 minutes or half an hour. Concentrate in the heart and repeat her name very fast, then no thoughts will come. If doubts come do not care but inwardly repeat, 'I am Mother's! I am Yours!' Continue to repeat her name. If you forget, then think to yourself 'Oh, I forgot!' And immediately start your japa anew.

All the adverse spirits and forces are very afraid of the Mother's name and cannot stay with a person who repeats the name with faith and dependence."

**Question**: But it is so difficult to always do japa!

**Babaji**: Yes, it is difficult. We must always try. If we continue trying, we will succeed. Always keep trying!

**Note**: Babaji said that this yoga, because of Nama-Japa, is infinitely easier than the old yogas. If we do japa then automatically we surrender, we aspire and we reject the wrong movements.

**Question**: Will all sadhaks eventually repeat the Mother's name?

**Babaji**: Yes, all will eventually repeat the Mother's name.

**Question**: There are those who work sincerely, but who only repeat her name at certain times during the day. What about those?

**Babaji:** They repeat the Mother's name only for a short time, because they do not understand its immense value and importance. If they understood it, then why would they repeat her name only for a short time? They would repeat it always.

## More from the sadhak's diary

Babaji was bending down towards me, listening to something I was telling. Suddenly he looked at me intently. Then, pointing his forefinger and sweeping his arm across the air in support of his words he said with great force:

"Have faith in THE NAME!"

It went through my whole being from top to bottom.

Babaji was telling us tirelessly to repeat the Mother's name always even at the time of getting dressed, taking a bath or brushing our teeth. He was encouraging us to repeat the name loudly when alone and silently in the mouth, using the lips at other times, as expressed by Sri Aurobindo so sweetly in his epic poem Savitri:

*A key to a Light still kept in being's core,*
*The sun-word of an ancient mystery's sense,*
*Her name ran murmuring on the lips of men*
*Exalted and sweet like an inspired verse*[38]

One day a sadhak told Babaji that if he repeated the Mother's name silently moving his lips, others would think that he has gone out of his mind, uttering things to himself. Babaji answered:

"So what! Let them think whatever they want! They will observe the way you live and they will begin to respect you. Eventually the day will come when they will realize what it means and they will follow your example. When one repeats the name it is as if the person is actually present. The name and the force of the person are one."

**Question:** Can one learn to increase one's concentration?

**Babaji:** Yes, Sri Aurobindo speaks about 3 centres of concentration. The heart, the third eye and the head.

**Question:** Inside the head or above?

**Babaji:** Better above, just above the head. In the beginning though it is better to try to concentrate in the heart. It is difficult to concentrate in the heart or above the head. At first one cannot do it. Then one should concentrate outside the heart. Keep an image of the Mother in front of you, concentrate on it and do japa. Gradually try to go deeper and imagine the picture in the heart. If one goes into the heart or above the head all thoughts will stop.

By meditating on the heart-centre the psychic aspiration will automatically grow. One has to be very determined, very determined! Have determination!

A sadhak was complaining about his difficulties in overcoming certain defects in his nature.

**Babaji:** You know, sadhana is not done in one day! Do you know this? (Yes, Babaji). It takes time! The mind, vital and body of a person do not want God. They want to control the person. When someone does sadhana, then the mind, vital and body are gradually being controlled by this person. They do not like this and throw up all lower movements to disturb the sadhak. They try to lure him away from the path by any means using all kinds of suggestions. At such times it is important not to listen to these suggestions and not to follow them. One has to offer them to the Mother and think that these disturbances have come up for transformation. These things are bound to come up, but do not care.

You know, if you are really sincere, Mother will do everything, arrange everything and you will know what to do!

**Note:** Babaji pointed out to us two books which are most important and with whose help we can practice this yoga.

*The Mother* by Sri Aurobindo and *Nama-Japa in the Yoga of Transformation*. Babaji asked us to learn the last paragraph of chapter 3 of *The Mother* by heart:

*"The more complete your faith, sincerity and surrender, the more will grace and protection be with you. And when the grace and protection of the Divine Mother are with you, what is there that can touch you or whom need you fear? A little of it even will carry you through all difficulties, obstacles and dangers; surrounded by its full presence you can go securely on your way because it is hers, careless of all menace, unaffected by any hostility however powerful, whether from this world or from worlds invisible. Its touch can turn difficulties into opportunities, failure into success and weakness into unfaltering strength. For the grace of the Divine Mother is the sanction of the Supreme and now or tomorrow its effect is sure, a thing decreed, inevitable and irresistible."*[39]

Babaji wrote a series of small books in Oriya explaining Sri Aurobindo's and the Mother's yoga, answering questions and giving advice of how to practise it. His aim was that even simple, uneducated people should understand this yoga and practise it. This series has been published in Oriya under the name of *Sri Aurobindo Loka Sahitya*. The book *Nama-Japa in the Yoga of Transformation* is the only book of this series so far which has been

translated and published in English because Babaji held it to be of utmost importance. On different occasions Babaji told several sadhaks who were close to him that actually he had not written any of the books of this series...
Before the publication of the English edition in 1994, it was read out to Babaji in his room. Babaji was listening intently like a small child with a beaming face, as if he heard the content of the book for the first time. There seemed to be no recollection of the fact that he himself had actually written the book.

Though in her lifetime Mother did say to some sadhaks to repeat her name, it is felt that she was far too humble to stress on this infallible help while still in her physical body.

Babaji said that the name 'Ma' contains the full power of the Supramental Force and Light. It is easy to repeat and connects us immediately with the Mother. Even in ordinary life, if a child cries for his mother, the mother of this child is bound to respond.

**Question:** Would it not be easier to withdraw from life for some time and concentrate and then come back once one has found the contact with one's soul?

**Babaji:** No! In the traditional yoga paths, mind, vital and body did not realize the divine. There remained a gulf between the lower and the higher existence, there was no possibility to connect these two. Only the Supramental Force which Sri Aurobindo and the Mother brought down to earth, will now connect the lower hemisphere with the higher hemisphere through the complete transformation of man's mind, vital and body. Previously this was not possible. In the traditional paths only a few people attained Mukti while the suffering of the world, disease, old age and death continued unabated.

While practising Sri Aurobindo's and the Mother's yoga, our lower nature will be illumined and divinised and eventually a life divine will be established upon earth.

If we go into seclusion, we may establish contact with our soul but neglect to change and transform our mind, vital and body. Only by living and working with others and facing life will the Psychic direct its influence on these parts and gradually turn them towards the Divine. If we live in seclusion, the difficulties of our mind, vital and body are not activated, they lie dormant, we simply neglect them and the Psychic in us will not transform them.

This yoga is an integral yoga, in the sense that all the parts of our being will have to be transformed. If, for example, only the mind progresses and goes too far ahead of the other parts of the being it will have to wait for the vital and physical to catch up. All parts have to advance together and we need each other to advance and grow.
The more people practise this sadhana the easier

it becomes for each one. It needs groups of people. The final transformation into Superman cannot be achieved by one person alone. It needs a small group. When a small group of people will be supramentalised it will affect the whole world. Pain and suffering will then stop, man will be happy. He may choose to do sadhana to evolve quickly or he may choose to evolve slowly in the course of evolution without doing sadhana.

We think that this yoga is difficult, but actually the old yoga paths were much more difficult. Their practitioners had to overcome so many obstacles, physical as well as psychological and through intense concentration and tapasya they separated their consciousness from their mind, vital and body and staged it in higher realms without being able to connect the lower with the higher. Only very few persons succeeded in doing so.

The traditional yogas were more difficult than this yoga because the sadhak had to rely on his own strength. In this yoga it is not at all possible to succeed by one's own strength. It is the Mother who will do this yoga through us and take up the transformation of our mind, vital and body until they too are able to express in life their true godly qualities.

In this integral yoga, everyone who truly accepts Mother and her ideal will progress and will eventually reach the goal. We think that we are suffering but people in ordinary life suffer much more than we do. Furthermore, if we constantly tell ourselves that things are difficult, they will be difficult! If, on the other hand, we feel that they are easy, they will become easy.

Satya Yuga, or the golden age of Truth, has already begun to manifest, but the asuric forces also have come up with full force trying to fight the Truth. Falsehood, however, will not be able to prevail against Truth.

An interesting question was posed with regard to the astras (special weapons) used in the great war of the Mahabharata.

**Question**: Were the astras that were used for fighting in the Mahabharata war used on the physical plane or some occult plane?

**Babaji:** They were real and used on the physical plane. At that time some people knew the mantras for using these weapons which were much more powerful than the nuclear weapons of today.

**Question**: Why are they not here anymore?

**Babaji:** You want to know why they are not here any longer? I will tell you. For everything there is a necessity. When the necessity is over the thing disappears. If we had those weapons now people would do such inhuman cruelties. Therefore the mantras to use these weapons are now lost.

**Question:** But we now have atomic weapons. They are also so cruel. Can one use a mantra to control them?

**Babaji:** A mantra is not necessary. For this the Supramental Force has come down to earth. Once Superman appears on earth he can easily control these weapons. But in the meantime the Supramental Force will not allow nuclear weapons to destroy the world. Man will not be able to use the atomic bomb.

The topic of mantras continued.

**Babaji:** In India there are mantras for all kinds of situations. There are mantras to cure diseases in humans as well as in animals. I myself experienced it. My mother and father knew a mantra which could cure a person who was bitten by a poisonous snake. In my village quite a number of people would get bitten by snakes.

When I was eight years old I found this mantra one day which was written on a palm leaf. When I read it I knew that it was the mantra to cure someone from a poisonous snake bite. I decided to memorize it. Then, one day they brought a person to our house who had been bitten by a cobra. My mother, father and my older brother were not at home. I was not sure whether the mantra would work and neither were the people, who had collected at our house, sure whether I could use it correctly.

I made a specific movement with my hand and said the mantra. The person was cured.

Laughingly Babaji continued:
I also knew a mantra of how to cure pain in one's hands and another one of how to kill a person who is far away. But to use any mantra you have to have a Siddhi, a Tapasya, otherwise the mantra will not work, it will be only words without power. When I became a sadhu I dropped all those mantras.

# Sweet Babaji Maharaj

When Babaji was in Ayodhya, he had written to the Ashram for permission to visit. In those days practically nobody was admitted via a letter, and especially aspirants of any traditional path were not given permission to come. But in Babaji's case it was all different. When the letter from the Ashram was on its way he felt it and knew that his permission was coming. The letter finally arrived and it contained a blessing packet. Babaji felt the force emanating from this blessing packet so strongly that for 3 days he was in constant bliss.

Babaji recounted several insightful stories:
**Note:** The person involved in these stories was no longer alive at the time, otherwise Babaji would not have told them.

Mother had set up a department which was focusing on spreading Sri Aurobindo's message throughout India and also abroad. Babaji was doing a similar work in the Indian state of Orissa. Experiencing numerous difficulties in their work, the head of the concerned department asked the Mother the following question:

"Mother, why is it that Babaji, who does a similar work as we do, always succeeds in what he is doing while we face endless difficulties, due to which our work is being held up. There are quarrels and disagreements among us or illnesses and other obstacles crop up, due to which our work is endlessly delayed. What is the secret of Babaji's success, Mother?"

Mother smiled and answered: "He knows a secret mantra."

X was very happy to hear this and immediately asked the Mother to reveal the mantra so that they too would succeed in their work. Mother again smiled and said:

"Why should I tell you, you can ask him yourself."

**Note**: Since Babaji had joined the Ashram after having already gained realisation in the traditional yoga he had been practising, X was convinced that the mantra Babaji was using was a powerful invocation which he must have learned during his previous yogic practices, realizing little that Babaji had surrendered all his inner knowledge, his mantra-practices and achievements at the Mother's feet when he came to the Ashram.

One day X met Babaji in order to hear from him this magic mantra, which seemed to give him success in all his undertakings. At the time Babaji was quietly sitting in his room doing Japa.

"Babaji, I want to ask you a question."

"Yes, I am right here, what is it that you want to ask?"

"No, no Babaji, it is very important. I cannot ask it here. Please come with me to my office."

Babaji was driven by car to X's private office wondering what important inquiry this could possibly be. Then came the crucial question:

"Babaji, please tell me the secret mantra you are using so I also can practice it."

Surprised, Babaji answered: "I do not have any secret mantra."

"Yes, yes Babaji, Mother said so. You have a secret mantra and this is the reason why you always succeed in whatever you are doing. Please tell me this mantra so that I may also use it."

Babaji replied:

"I do not have any secret mantra. The only thing that I am doing is this: I repeat the Mother's name 'Ma' continuously without stopping."

The same person from the above story, who had frequent physical contact with the Mother, asked her the following question:

"Mother, how is it that Babaji never asks your permission before undertaking any work while we always have to ask your permission for any work we want to do?"

Mother smiled and answered:

"He always asks me permission for everything he is doing!"

Babaji had a fully conscious inner contact with the Mother.

Babaji joined the Ashram in 1945 after having already gained the realisations of the "old yoga". Even at that time he was already recognized as being a great saint and yogi. Sometime after Babaji had settled in the Sri Aurobindo Ashram visitors started to come from his home state, Orissa, to meet him and find out why he had come to Pondicherry and what this special yoga here was all about.

A small group of people had arrived from Orissa and asked Babaji about Sri Aurobindo's yoga. They wanted to know the difference between this yoga and the traditional yogic methods which everyone knew about. Babaji, being of a very humble and sweet predisposition, thought to himself: "Why will I tell them myself, I am not a great scholar, let me send them to one of the great learned persons at the Ashram. They will be much better able to explain Sri Aurobindo's yoga to them than I..."

So Babaji sent his visitors to one of the Ashram lecturers. In the evening time after having met this person the visitors from Orissa again collected in Babaji's room. Babaji was happy to see them and asked them very sweetly:

"Well, now do you understand what this yoga is?"
"Oh no, Babaji," came the surprising answer, "this yoga is not for us! We were told that this yoga is

like fire, that it is extremely difficult and should not be attempted. We were told that this yoga will burn us if we do not have the true inner call. No, Babaji, let us stay with our Lord Jaganath in Puri, this yoga is much too difficult for us!"

Babaji was deeply surprised and from this very moment inwardly resolved to never send away anyone who would ask him about this yoga. Then he said:

"Now, listen to me. I will explain this yoga to you." Everyone listened attentively.

"On one hand this yoga is the most difficult of all yoga paths."

"Yes, yes", came the enthusiastic reply, "that's what we were told."

Babaji continued:

"But on the other hand, this yoga is the easiest of all." Everyone looked at Babaji in disbelief. How could it possibly be the most difficult and the easiest path at the same time?

Babaji:
"It is the most difficult yoga because it has never been done before. The transformation of mind, life and body has never been done in the past. But on the other hand it is the easiest of all, because in this yoga it is not by one's own tapasya that one succeeds, it is the Mother herself who does the yoga

in us and through us. The only thing necessary for us is to feel ourselves to be a little child sitting in the lap of the Mother. Think that all you are and all you have belongs to the Mother. Think that 'Mother will always take care of me and protect me'. Surrender yourself in her lap like a little child and always repeat her name, 'Ma'. If you can do this much, the Mother herself will do this yoga for you."

There was great happiness since everyone present felt that in this way the practice of this special integral yoga was quite possible even for them.

**Note:** Due to Babaji's influence Sri Aurobindo's yoga is practised in Orissa with great fervour. At present (2023) there are more than 10,000 study circles, over 500 integral schools and 73 relic centres in this one Indian state alone.

Babaji had fallen and an x-ray revealed a small crack in a lower vertebra. He was advised complete bed-rest for 2 to 3 weeks. Reluctantly he followed the order. After ONE day in bed he pronounced that now he had listened enough to the doctors and wasn't going to listen anymore and that the Mother's name alone would set everything right.

In the evening Babaji was sitting as usual in his chair and when he was asked whether he had any pain, he replied that there was no crack. When someone asked him if it was necessary to consult doctors and take medicines, Babaji said: "If a person is doing sadhana sincerely and is repeating the Mother's name, no doctors and medicines are necessary, the Mother's name alone will do everything.

At this point a person remarked that since Babaji was repeating the Mother's name the accident should not have happened in the first place. Babaji replied that Mother had saved him and that this little physical difficulty which he had to face was in order to make that part of the body more strong and conscious, it was for progress.

Prior to coming to the Ashram, Babaji was staying at Ayodhya in his guru's ashram and was one of his personal attendants. The primary work of all the sadhaks was to do japa of Ram-Nam, to study the Ramayan and to be engaged in devotional discussions. Babaji felt more inclined towards japa, which he had been doing since his childhood. There were large numbers of devotees coming to the ashram quite frequently and Babaji had to spend some time with them, which naturally interrupted the flow of his continuous japa. In order to be able to practice his japa without interruption, Babaji decided to shift to an abandoned shed, some distance away from his guru's ashram. One of Babaji's fellow sadhaks agreed to bring their guru's prasad to Babaji daily and another devotee offered a nourishing drink consisting of milk and almonds every day.

**Question:** Babaji, you had no work, so what were

you doing there?

**Babaji:** Nama-Japa.

**Question:** Excluding about 7 to 8 hours spent towards sleep and your daily personal chores, were you doing only japa for the remaining 16 or 17 hours of the day?

Babaji smiled so sweetly and said:
"Ah! It was giving me so much of Ananda! I was thinking that if japa done by just one person with only one tongue can give so much Ananda, how much Ananda would there be if a thousand tongues would repeat the name! The Ananda from the japa was so intense that in spite of feeling hungry and seeing the prasad in front of me I hesitated to take it because japa would have to be stopped, which would then cause a decrease in Ananda for the duration of eating. The same thing happened with the delicious drink which was standing in front of me and which I hesitated to drink in spite of being thirsty. I did not want to interrupt this continuous flow of Ananda from the repetition of the name.

After some time a sadhu taught me how to do japa at every hair-root of the entire body. I practised this and had the Ananda, but there was a danger because during the japa the body would rise quite a bit above the ground and would then suddenly drop back down. Therefore, after about one and a half years, I discontinued this practice."

**Question:** After discontinuing this special method

and coming back to your old original way of doing japa did you get back the same Ananda as you felt before?

**Babaji:** No, this was no longer possible, because the effect of Sri Aurobindo's yoga had already started to work in the earth atmosphere.

**Note:** Babaji Ramkrishna Das, stayed at Ayodhya for about 16 years doing the sadhana of Nama-Japa. Then the Divine changed his course of sadhana and he came to the Sri Aurobindo Ashram in 1945. After many years of stay in Pondicherry, when numerous people started visiting him, he began to ponder whether in this Integral Yoga also he should ask the visitors to do Nama-Japa. After studying the Mother's Agenda and also finding references to the practice of Nama-Japa at different places in Sri Aurobindo's writings and through his own inner realisation, Babaji was finally convinced that in this yoga also, Nama-Japa is essential for the transformation of the body.

It was especially during the last 20 years of his life that Babaji started writing in each and every of his numerous correspondences with devotees from Orissa, to have an unshakable faith and dependence on the Mother and to constantly do japa of the Mother's name. Year after year he wrote thousands of letters to devotees giving advice and responding to questions of sadhaks in all fields of life, always stressing the importance of Ma-Nama-Japa. Babaji felt that Nama-Japa done by so many people would create a wide, solid and raised platform of general consciousness, which in turn would help the more advanced sadhaks to rise still higher and thereby accelerate the process of transformation.

Perhaps the response was not up to what Babaji had hoped for, and early in the year of 1998 (he left his body in November of the same year), he thought of creating a base of Nama-Japa around himself. At that time, due to some physical difficulties, Babaji was getting up only at about 5 o'clock in the morning. Two persons were staying with him at night and another 3 were coming early morning to help him with his morning chores.

It was the early morning of March 23, 1998 that Babaji got up at 5 am and immediately sat on his low chair. Looking at his attendants he said: "Today, instead of the usual routine, we shall do Nama-Japa."

The 5 attendants sat down, Babaji started repeating "Ma, Ma, Ma, Ma...." with a loud voice and others started to join in. Babaji stopped after half an hour. It was then decided to do the japa every day from 5 am to 5:30 am, and throughout the day Babaji repeated this several times. The morning japa continued for the next 2 days. On the second day Babaji announced that this morning japa would from now on also be done in the evening time from 6:30 pm to 7:00 pm. It was started the same day.

As the information spread many people started joining the japa sessions especially in the evening. After some time Babaji started distributing banana-prasad with his own hands to those who attended the evening japa. Those bananas tasted like nectar. Gradually Babaji's physical condition deteriorated and he was not able to leave his bed, yet the japa-sessions continued.

On August 16th, 1998, two days after his birthday, sometime during the morning hours, Babaji was admitted to the Ashram Nursing Home. During his stay of 89 days at the Nursing Home, the japa-sessions continued in Babaji's room at 5 in the morning and at 6:30 in the evening. Babaji had given instructions for these sessions in his room to continue and this was done accordingly despite oppositions and hindrances. Towards the later part of Babaji's stay at the Nursing Home Ma-Nama-Japa was done continuously in Babaji's own room from 5 am to 9 pm every day. This was appreciated by Babaji.

In the Nursing Home he was at times answering a few questions and was saying that his physical transformation was still possible. On the 16th of September during a brief discussion, Babaji said:

"The higher nature has already achieved victory over the lower nature, but it has not yet gained victory over the physical body. This will definitely be done and one will not have to leave the body. Nama-Japa and surrender are necessary for this victory. There will be no necessity of doctors and treatments. These are necessary only for one's mental satisfaction."

A few days before he left his body he was questioned:

**Question**: Babaji, is it still possible that your body can be transformed?

**Babaji**: No, this time it is not possible.

**Question**: Why, Babaji? You had said that your body was ready for the transformation.

**Babaji**: There was a short pause, then Babaji said: "Nama-Japa could not be done properly."

By this time he had almost stopped talking and was always keeping his eyes closed. But whenever anybody was doing japa of the Mother's name at his bed-side he opened his eyes and looked in that direction without blinking. This was being noticed almost till the crucial day of 8.11.1998, the day he left his body.

While he was in the Ashram Nursing Home he would go into trance. On one particular day, with the help of two attendants Babaji was sitting up in his bed, slowly looking from side to side. It was evident that he was not seeing us at all but was seeing something of the Supramental World. His eyes were completely indrawn so that only the white of the eyes was visible. As he continued to move his head very slowly from left to right and right to left, obviously observing something, he began to speak slowly in Oriya. His voice seemed to come from very far away: "Like this it will be! Like this it will be! The road is wide and clear, Nama-Japa is the only way."

# The Mother and Sri Aurobindo on Nama-Japa

"We must erase the imprint little by little. And in fact, the only way to erase the imprint is to make contact with the Truth. There is no other way – all reasoning, all intelligence, all understanding, all that is totally useless with this physical mind. The only thing is to make contact. That's just what the cells value: the possibility of making contact.
Making contact.
On the material level, japa is very good for that. When your head is tired and you are a little weary of forever contradicting that pessimism, you just have to repeat your japa, and automatically you make contact. To make contact. That's something the cells value a lot. A lot. It's a very good way, because it's a way that isn't mental, it's a mechanical way, it's a question of vibration."[40]

"....Now where does japa fit into all this?
Japa, like meditation, is a procedure – apparently the most active and effective procedure – for joining, as much as possible, the Divine Presence to the bodily substance. It is the magic of sound, you see.

Naturally, if there's also an awareness of the idea behind it, if one does japa as a very active CONSCIOUS invocation, then its effects are greatly multiplied. But the basis is the magic of sound. This is a fact of experience, and it's absolutely true. The sound OM,

*for instance, awakens very special vibrations (there are other such sounds as well, but of course that one is the most powerful of all).*
*It is an attempt to divinize material substance.*
*From another, almost identical point of view, it fills the physical atmosphere with the Divine Presence. So time spent in japa is time consecrated to helping the material substance enter into more intimate rapport with the Divine."*[41]

"*Only on the heart's veiled door the word of flame*
*Is written, the secret and tremendous Name.*"[42]

# Japa and Science

In his book *Nama-Japa in the Yoga of Transformation*, Babaji Ramkrishna Das emphasises the importance of Nama-Japa for the physical transformation, because only japa has a direct influence on the cells of the body.

Interestingly, the effect of sound on matter has been demonstrated in a straightforward and fascinating manner by the Japanese scientist Masaru Emoto.

Emoto started with the premises that water was one of the main building blocks of life. About 70% of our earth is covered by water. Similarly, about 70% of the human body consists of water. Though all types of water look alike to our naked eye, Emoto presupposed that the inherent nature contained in water must differ for various kinds of water sources. Through the advancement of science we are now able to quite easily demonstrate the different grades of pollution within a given water sample and can pronounce a source of water as 'dead' or 'alive'. But does water have a nature and consciousness of its own, and if yes, how to make this visible to the human eye?

Emoto had an ingenious idea. He froze water and took photographs of the resulting crystal formations of the same water. The results were astounding and fascinating. Testing water samples from various sources from all over the world (tap water, river water, lake water, spring water, distilled water etc.),

Emoto found that the healthier the water, the more beautiful the crystal formations. Polluted water did not form any crystals or formed only partial crystals, depending on the degree of pollution.

Emoto had succeeded to show that water was carrying information which could be made visible through crystallization. He suspected that water has a consciousness which responds to thoughts, words, music, ideas and prayers etc. To prove this he used a controlled sample of distilled water because he found that distilled water had the least impurities and when frozen formed a simple crystal structure. After taking pictures of distilled water crystals he exposed the same water to various stimuli such as collective thoughts and concentration upon a given water sample, classical music, folk music, heavy metal music, words, names, names of gods, prayers and japa.

Emoto was able to demonstrate the same results consistently:

Water responded to the various stimuli it was exposed to. The more positive the energy with which the water had been confronted the more wonderful the crystal formations. Distilled water which was exposed to heavy metal music, or ugly negative words, did not form any crystals at all. Quite to the contrary, the original simple crystal structure of the distilled water sample was completely broken up into pieces after having been exposed to these negative stimuli. On the other hand, distilled water exposed to positive stimuli such as classical music, kind words and prayers, formed beautiful crystals when frozen.

Emoto has clearly shown in his research that water has a consciousness which responds to environmental stimuli. He writes that *"the vibrations of music and words transmitted through air effect water more than any other element"*.[43] Water exposed to prayer and japa, for example, produced the most marvelous and astounding crystal structures.

Can we begin to imagine the wonderful results possible, if we exposed our human body to the constant and conscious repetition of the Mother's Name?

# References

CWM = Collected Works of the Mother

SABCL = Sri Aurobindo Birth Centenary Library

1 The Mother, *Questions and Answers*, CWM, vol. 3, p. 26

2 *Mother's Agenda*, 1951-60, vol. l, p. 301

3 Sri Aurobindo, *On Himself*, SABCL, vol. 26, p. 511

4 Sri Aurobindo, *The Synthesis of Yoga*, SABCL, vol. 20, p. 75

5 Sri Aurobindo, *Letters on Yoga*, SABCL, vol. 23, p. 745

6 *Ibid.*, p. 746

7 *Ibid.*, p. 746

8 Sri Aurobindo, *The Synthesis of Yoga*, SABCL, vol. 20, p. 155

9 Sri Aurobindo, *On Himself*, SABCL, vol. 26, p. 512

10 Sri Aurobindo, *Savitri*, SABCL, vol. 28, p. 210 (Book 2, Canto 7)

11 *Ibid.*, p. 232 (Book 2, Canto 8)

12 Sri Aurobindo, *Savitri*, SABCL 1970, vol. 29, p. 366 (Book 4, Canto 2)

13 *Ibid.*, p. 383 (Book 4, Canto 4)

14 Sri Aurobindo, *On Himself*, SABCL, vol. 26, p. 512

15 The Mother, Sri Aurobindo Ashram message of 17th November, 1993

16 Sri Aurobindo, *On Himself*, SABCL, vol. 26, p. 511

17 *Mother's Agenda*, 1951-60, vol. l, p. 301

18 *Ibid.*, p. 301

19 Sri Aurobindo, *On Himself*, SABCL, vol. 26, p. 511

20 The Mother, *On Education*, CWM, vol. 12, p. 449

21 Sri Aurobindo, *The Mother*, SABCL, vol. 25, p. 6

22 Sri Aurobindo, *Essays on the Gita*, Sri Aurobindo Ashram Trust, 1972, Bhagavad Gita, chapter IX, verse 2

23 The Mother, *Questions and Answers*, CWM, vol. 3, p. 1

24 *Mother's Agenda*, 1951-60, vol. 1, p. 301

25 *Ibid.*, pp. 420-21

26 *Ibid.*, p. 356

27 *Ibid.*, p. 301

28 *Ibid.*, p. 301

29 *Mother's Agenda*, Vol. 2, p. 97, 196

30 CWSA Volume 23, *The Synthesis of Yoga*, p.8, 1999

31 CWSA Volume 36, *Autobiographical Notes and Other Writings of Historical Interest*, p. 369, 2006

32 CWSA Volume 13, *Essays in Philosophy and Yoga*, pp. 546, 547, 1998

33 CWSA Volume 13, *Essays in Philosophy and Yoga: The Divine Body*, p. 536, 1998

34 CWSA Volume 32, *The Mother with Letters on the Mother*, p. 3, 2012

35 CWSA Volume 32, *The Mother with Letters on the Mother*, p. 3, 2012

36 CWSA Volume 32, *The Mother with Letters on the Mother*, p. 3, 2012

37 CWSA Volume 32, *The Mother with Letters on the Mother*, pp. 8, 9, 2012

38 SABCL 1970, vol. 29, *Savitri*, p. 366

39 CWSA Volume 32, *The Mother with Letters on the Mother*, pp. 8, 9, 2012

40 *Mother's Agenda*, vol. 5, p. 232, Oct. 10th, 1964

41 *Mother's Agenda*, vol. 3, p. 69, Feb. 3rd, 1962

42 CWSA Volume 2, *Collected Poems*, p. 607, 2009

43 Masaru Emoto, *Messages from Water*, p. 72, 2009

# Glossary

*The terms below are defined in Sri Aurobindo's words as far as possible.*

**Acharya** teacher

**Adhara** support, receptacle; the mind, vital and body of the sadhak, the mental-vital-physical system as a vessel of the spiritual consciousness

**Agni** fire, spiritual fire

**Agni-bija** seed-syllable for agni (see also 'bija')

**Ananda** spiritual bliss, delight; the essential principle of delight

**Antaratma** inner self, soul

**Ashram** a spiritual community, a place where sadhana is practised under a spiritual master

**Asuric** pertaining to hostile, anti-divine forces (asuras)

**Avatar** an incarnation of the Divine in a human body

**Bhakti** love and devotion for the Divine, the delight of the heart in God

**Bija** in the theory of mantra, certain syllables embody and invoke particular spiritual powers; these single syllables are termed seed-syllables

**Brahmic Consciounsness** pertaining to the Brahman, the one Reality or Absolute

**Buddhi** intellect, the mental power of understanding and discrimination

**Mantra** a mystical formula, usually composed of Sanskrit letters and words having a spiritual significance and power

**Matrishakti** the Power of the Mother

**Mukti** salvation; liberation from the Ignorance and the cycle of birth and death

**Muni** a sage

**Nama-japa** the repetition of the name of the Divine. In this book it refers to the constant repetition of the Mother's name, *Ma*

**Nirvana** extinction, cessation of the being as we know it. Nirvana is a liberated condition of the being, not a world; it is a withdrawal from the worlds and the manifestation

**Psychic being** the evolving soul of the individual, the divine portion in him which evolves from life to life. The psychic being supports the mind, life and body, aiding their growth and development; its characteristic power is to turn everything to the Divine

**Purana** a class of Indian spiritual literature

**Rishi** a seer, a sage, usually associated with the Vedic and Upanishadic periods

**Sachchidananda (sat-chit-ananda)** literally Existence (sat), Consciousness (chit), Bliss (ananda); a formula used to describe the Supreme Reality

**Sadhak** one who practises spiritual discipline, one who is getting or trying to get spiritual realisation

**Sadhana** spiritual discipline or practice; the practice of yoga; the practice by which perfection (siddhi) is attained

**Samadhi** in this context, the marble tomb of Sri Aurobindo

**Sannyasi** ascetic, one who has renounced the worldly life

**Shakti** Power, Energy; the Power of the Mother

**Shastras** scriptures, sacred writings

**Supramental** the Supramental is the Truth-Consciousness, the highest Divine Consciousness and Force operating in the universe, and what it brings in its descent is the full truth of life, the full truth of consciousness in Matter

**Upanishads** a class of Sanskrit sacred writings

**Vedas** the most ancient of the Indian spiritual scriptures

**Vital** the Life-nature made up of desires, sensations, feelings, passions, energies of action, will of desire, reactions of the desire-soul in man and of all that play of possessive and other related instincts, anger, fear, greed, lust, etc., that belong to this field of the nature.

**Yoga** union with the Divine; the practice that leads to this union

**Yoga of Transformation** Sri Aurobindo's Yoga, which aims at the divinisation of the entire nature of man and a divine life on earth

**Yoga-shakti** yoga-power

**Yogi** one who has attained union with the Divine

"... the Mantra which is chosen for Japa has the necessary power within it and by constant repetition under proper conditons the power can be evoked into operation to effectuate the purpose. The vibrations set up each time the Mantra is repeated go to create, in the subtler atmosphere, the conditions that induce the fulfilment of the object in view. The Divine Name, for instance, has the potency to stamp and mould the consciousness which repeats it into the nature of the Divinity for which the Name stands and prepare it for the reception of the gathering Revelation of the Godhead."

M.P. Pandit, Japa,

2000, p. 9

"A key to a Light still kept in being's core, The sun-word of an ancient mystery's sense, Her name ran murmuring on the lips of men Exalted and sweet like an inspired verse..."

Sri Aurobindo

"It was during those days in our Ashram when the Mother was giving Blessings daily in the mornings to all the inmates and the visitors present. The number was about a thousand and all used to go in a queue and receive Her Blessings individually, the whole function taking nearly an hour. One day a young girl who had taken to the Japa of the Mother's Name as part of her sadhana, found the Mantra MOTHER, MOTHER, MOTHER, repeating itself spontaneously in her heart while she was standing in the queue. There were at least twenty persons ahead of her. Imagine her surprise when she beheld the Mother taking off Her eyes from those in front and looking straight at her who was standing at such a distance! The Call of the Mantra had obviously reached the Mother and She had instantly responded even physically."

M.P. Pandit, Japa

2000, p. 7/8

# International Publications

**Auroville Architecture**
*by Franz Fassbender*

**Auroville Form Style and Design**
*by Franz Fassbender*

**Landscapes and Gardens of Auroville**
*by Franz Fassbender*

**Inauguration of Auroville**
*by Franz Fassbender*

**Auroville in a Nutshell**
*by Tim Wrey*

**Death doesn't exist**
The Mother on Death, Sri Aurobindo on Rebirth
*Compiled by Franz Fassbender*

**Divine Love**
*Compiled by Franz Fassbender*

**Five Dream**
*by Sri Aurobindo*

**A Vision**
*Compiled by Franz Fassbender*

**Passage to More than India**
*by Dick Batstone*

**The Mother on Japan**
*Compiled by Franz Fassbender*

**Children of Change: A Spiritual Pilgrimage**
*by Amrit (Howard Shoji Iriyama)*

**Memories of Auroville - told by early Aurovilians**
*by Janet Feran*

**The Journeying Years**
*by Dianna Bowler*

**Auroville Reflected**
*by Bindu Mohanty*

**Finding the Psychic Being**
*by Loretta Shartsis*

**The Teachings of Flowers**
The Life and Work of the Mother of the Sri Aurobindo Ashram
*by Loretta Shartsis*

**The Supramental Transformation**
*by Loretta Shartsis*

**The Mother's Yoga - 1956-1973 (English & French)
Vol. 1, 1956-1967 & Vol. 2, 1968-1973**
*by Loretta Shartsis*

**Antithesis of Yoga**
*by Jocelyn Janaka*

**Bougainvilleas PROTECTION**
*by Narad (Richard Eggenberger), Nilisha Mehta*

**Crossroad The New Humanity**
*by Paulette Hadnagy*

**Die Praxis Des Integralen Yoga**
*by M. P. Pandit*

**The Way of the Sunlit Path**
*by William Sullivan*

**Wildlife great and small of India's Coromandel**
*by Tim Wrey*

**A New Education With A Soul**
*by Marguerite Smithwhite*

# Featured Titles

## Divine Love

The texts presented in this book are selected from the Mother and Sri Aurobindo.

"Awakened to the meaning of my heart. That to feel love and oneness is to live. And this the magic of our golden change, is all the truth I know or seek, O sage."

Sri Aurobindo, Savitri, Book XII, Epilog

## A Vision by the Mother

On 28th May 1958, the Mother recounted a vision she once had of a wonderful Being of Love and Consciousness, emanated from the Supreme Origin and projected directly into the Inconscient so that the creation would gradually awaken to the Supramental Consciousness. The Mother's account of this vision was brought out a first time in November 1906, in the Revue Cosmique, a monthly review published in Paris.

## A Dream – Aims and Ideals of Auroville
### the Mother on Auroville

50 years of Auroville from 28.02.1968 - 28.02.2018

Today, information about Auroville is abundant. Many people try to make meaning out of Auroville – about its conception, to what direction should we grow towards, and, what are we doing here?

But what was Mother's original Dream and what was her Vision for Auroville back then?

## Matrimandir Talks by the Mother

This book presents most of Mother's Matrimandir talks, including how she conceived the idea for this special concentration and meditation building in Auroville.

## Memories of Auroville - Told by early Aurovilians

Memories of Auroville is a book about the very early days of Auroville based on interviews made in 1997 with Aurovilians who lived here between 1968 and 1973. The interviews presented in this book are part of a history program for newcomers that I had created with my friend, Philip Melville in 1997. The plan was to divide Auroville's history into different eras and then interview Aurovilians according to their area of knowledge. Our first section would cover the years from 1968 till 1973 when the Mother was still in her physical body.

## The Way of the Sunlit Path

May The Way of the Sunlit Path be a convenient guide for activating this ancient truth as a support for a Conscious Evolution.
May it illumine the transformation offered to us in the Integral Yoga.

## A Dream Takes Shape (in English, French, Hindi)

A comprehensive brochure on the international township of Auroville in, ranging from its Charter and "Why Auroville?" to the plan of the township, the central Matrimandir, the national pavilions and residences, to working groups, the economy, making visits, how to join, its relationship to the Sri Aurobindo Ashram, and its key role in the future of the world. This brochure endeavours to highlight how The Mother envisioned Auroville from its inception, some of the major achievements realised over the years, and some of the difficulties currently faced in implementing the guidelines which she gave.

## Mother on Japan

I had everything to learn in Japan. For four years, from an artistic point of view, I lived from wonder to wonder. And everything in this city, in this country, from beginning to end, gives you the impression of impermanence, of the unexpected, the exceptional... ...everything in this city, in this country, from beginning to end, gives you the impression of impermanence, of the unexpected, the exceptional. You always come to things you did not expect; you want to find them again and they are lost – they have made something else which is equally charming.

## Auroville Reflected

On 28 February 1968, on an impoverished plateau on the Coromandel Coast of South India, about 4,000 people from around the world gathered for a most unusual inauguration. Handfuls of soil from the countries of the world were mixed together as a symbol of human unity. Why did Indira Gandhi, the erstwhile Prime Minister of India, support this development for "a city the earth needs?" Why did UNESCO endorse this project? Why does the Dalai Lama continue to be involved in the project? What led anthropologist Margaret Mead to insist that records must be kept of its progress? Why did both historian William Irwin Thompson and United Nations representative Robert Muller note that this social experiment may be a breakthrough for humanity even as critics commented, "it is an impossible dream"?

## A House For the Third Millennium
Essays on Matrimandir

Nightwatch at the Matrimandir...
A cosmic spectacle; the black expanse above, the big black crater of Matrimandir's excavation carved deep into the soil. The four pillars - two of which are completed and the other two nearing completion - are four huge ships coming together from the four corners of the earth to meet at this pro propitious spot...

## Passage to More than India

This book is a voyage of discovery. In 1959 the author, Dick Batstone, a classically educated bookseller in England, with a Christian background, comes across a life of the great Indian polymath Sri Aurobindo, though a series of apparently fortuitous circumstances. A meeting in Durham, England, leads him to a determination to get to the Sri Aurobindo Ashram in Pondicherry, a former French territory south of Madras.

www.ingramcontent.com/pod-product-compliance
Lightning Source LLC
LaVergne TN
LVHW010328070526
838199LV00065B/5687